TABLE-TOP SCIENCE:
INTERMEDIATE

FREMONT AREA
DISTRICT LIBRARY

Made possible through a grant from The Fremont Area Foundation

About the Author
Linda Allison is the author of many books
for children, including *The Reasons for Seasons* and
Blood and Guts.

Publisher: Roberta Suid
Editor: Carol Whiteley
Design & Production: Scott McMorrow

Entire contents copyright © 1997 by Monday Morning Books, Inc.
Box 1680, Palo Alto, CA 94302

For a complete catalog, please write to the address above,
or visit our Web site: www.mondaymorningbooks.com
e-mail: MMBooks@aol.com

Monday Morning is a registered trademark of
Monday Morning Books, Inc.

Permission is hereby granted to reproduce
student materials in this book for non-commercial
individual or classroom use.

ISBN 1-57612-019-8

Printed in the United States of America
987654321

CONTENTS

INTRODUCTION — 5

HEAT

1. **HOT OR NOT?** testing your temperature perception — 10
2. **HEAT DETECTIVE** using a liquid crystal thermometer — 12
3. **BOTTLE THERMOMETER** making a simple liquid thermometer — 14
4. **HOT ATOMS** a demonstration of molecular action — 15
5. **POPCORN BALLS** phase changes and heat make a sweet treat — 17
6. **INTERESTING DEGREES** understanding temperature change — 20
7. **CONDUCTOR TESTS** testing how heat travels — 24
8. **THE COOLEST KID** testing body temperature — 26
9. **DAILY DEGREES** exploring body temperature changes — 28
10. **YOUR HOT SPOTS** mapping heat differences on your body — 30
11. **COOLING SWEAT** seeing how evaporation keeps you cool — 32
12. **IS HOT PINK HOT?** looking for a cool color — 34

GLOSSARY — 36

CELLS

HELPFUL HINTS using the microscope — 38

1. **LOW-POWERED MAGNIFIERS** using a simple microscope — 41
2. **HOW BIG?** understanding scale — 43
3. **HIGH-POWER SCOPE** using a high-power microscope — 48
4. **CORK CELLS** studying cell walls — 51
5. **ONION SKIN** viewing living plant cells — 52
6. **ELODEA** learning the secret of green plants — 54
7. **EEK! CHEEK CELLS** viewing animal cells — 55
8. **ONE-CELLED ANIMALS** studying life in pond water — 57
9. **YEAST** observing the life cycle of yeast — 58
10. **CELL CITY** learning about body cells — 59

GLOSSARY — 60

FORCES

1. **BALANCING ACT** building a desktop sculpture	64
2. **SEESAW SCIENCE** finding out if same weights balance	66
3. **FIND YOUR CENTER** a nifty way to find the center of gravity	68
4. **FIENDISH FILM CAN** three stunts about gravity	70
5. **CRASH TESTING** investigating the topple point	74
6. **TIPSY TRIANGLE** can you stand a triangle on its tip?	76
7. **A BALANCED LUNCH** balancing acts with fruits and vegetables	78
8. **FLYING CAT** building an amazing balance toy	81
9. **ACROBAT** making a clothespin sculpture	82
10. **FALLING BODIES** uncovering the physics of falling bodies	83
11. **BUMPER SLUMPER** learning about friction	85
12. **FRICTION TESTING** friction and learning about inertia	88
13. **INERTIA CHALLENGES** amazing stunts at stations	90
14. **THE GREAT SLOW RACE** experimenting with a slope	94
GLOSSARY	96

Introduction

Table-Top Science is a hands-on set of explorations where everyone gets a chance to be the scientist—even the teacher. Each of the book's three units is organized around a theme: heat and temperature, cells, and forces. Each activity is meant to be a short exploration of the topic, much of which children can do themselves. Adult participation will be necessary for activities that call for demonstrations or that involve cooking, cutting, or using heat sources.

Each unit's activities build on each other and are best done in order. However, they may be done separately or used out of order. Activities can be left out if there isn't time, if they don't seem appropriate, or if their focus isn't of interest (science should never be boring!). No doubt you will have your own ideas, too; feel free to add activities to any unit.

The scientific method the explorations follow is presented in an informal way. It is, simply, make a guess, then make a test, then see what happened. Recording sheets are provided for some experiments. When questions present themselves, make up experiments and try to get the answers using the scientific method. **Remember that science is a process, not a result.**

Most of the materials the children will need should be easy to obtain. A list of special materials and equipment that are needed for some of the activities follows.

As the children investigate and explore, encourage them to have fun—and remind them that **in science there are no failed experiments!**

Activities

Each activity will include some or all of the following parts:

IDEAS TO THINK ABOUT

Questions to get the children started; things to consider; prompts to help the children find out what they know, what they don't know, and what they would like to know.

EXPERIMENT

This section asks the children to:
1. Make a hypothesis (the big scientific word for "guess").
2. Test their guess.
3. See what happened.

They might end up with a conclusion but very likely discover some things that lead to more questions.

MORE TO EXPLORE

More questions to pursue if there is time, or time for a child to explore his or her own questions.

WHAT'S HAPPENING

This section offers explanations, background concepts, and vocabulary definitions.

AMAZING FACTS

Special bits of information that add to the investigation.

EXTENSIONS

Related activities to try in other subject areas, and family activities to do at home.

Special Materials

"HEAT" ACTIVITIES:

1. HOT OR NOT?: ice water, hot tap water, room-temperature water, three bowls, blindfold, towel
2. HEAT DETECTIVE: liquid crystal thermometer cards
3. BOTTLE THERMOMETER: pop bottles, drinking straws, corks or plasticene clay, food coloring
4. HOT ATOMS: two clear bottles, ice water, very hot water, food coloring, presweetened Kool-Aid powder, clear cups, sugar, ice
5. POPCORN BALLS: popcorn, pan and oil or popcorn popper, sugar, white corn syrup, salt, vinegar, big pot with lid, candy thermometer, measuring cups and spoons, hot plate or stove, margarine, spoon, towels
6. INTERESTING DEGREES: temperature cards, pushpins
7. CONDUCTOR TESTS: candle, matches, test rods, marbles, artist's wax, cardboard, testing strips such as brass, copper, glass, and wood
8. THE COOLEST KID: strip thermometers
9. DAILY DEGREES: strip thermometers
10. YOUR HOT SPOTS: strip thermometers
11. COOLING SWEAT: plastic bags, rubbing alcohol, cotton balls, blindfold, cups
12. IS HOT PINK HOT?: outdoor thermometer

"CELLS" ACTIVITIES:

1. LOW-POWERED MAGNIFIERS: simple microscope, magazines, cardboard
2. HOW BIG?: paper puzzle pieces, envelopes, drawing paper
3. HIGH-POWER SCOPE: high-power microscope
4. CORK CELLS: high-power microscope, cork, razor blade, water, slides, cover slips, eyedropper
5. ONION SKIN: high-power microscope, mat knife, onion, slides, eyedropper, iodine, cover slips
6. ELODEA: high-power microscope, slides, cover slips, Elodea leaves (available in fish stores; also known as Anacharis), water, eyedropper

7. EEK! CHEEK CELLS: high-power microscope, toothpick or tongue depressor, slides, iodine, cover slips, eyedropper, needle
8. ONE-CELLED ANIMALS: high-power microscope, slides, cover slips, eyedropper, pond water (or sea water or fish tank water)
9. YEAST: package of dry yeast, warm water, sugar, salt, balloons, clean pop bottles, spoon, funnel, bowl, measuring cup and spoons

"FORCES" ACTIVITIES:

1. BALANCING ACT: plastic straws, pushpins, clay, hole punch
2. SEESAW SCIENCE: balance beam, block, large paper clips, nail, clay (if needed)
3. FIND YOUR CENTER: washers, string, pushpins, cardboard, ruler
4. FIENDISH FILM CAN: film can, straight-back chair, paper money
5. CRASH TESTING: typing paper, notebook paper, rubber bands, construction materials such as tape, cardboard, etc.
6. TIPSY TRIANGLE: cardboard
7. A BALANCED LUNCH: assorted fruits and vegetables, toothpicks, kitchen items, coat hanger wire, pliers
8. FLYING CAT: lightweight cardboard, coins, string, cat shape
9. ACROBAT: pinch clothespin, wire (16-18 gauge), plasticene clay, pliers, small weights, wire cutter
10. FALLING BODIES: an orange and a grapefruit or light and heavy balls such as a tennis ball and a bowling ball
11. BUMPER SLUMPER: dowel, wire, wire cutter, plasticine clay, cardboard, odds and ends (wiggly or noisy things to attach such as a film can filled with beans, colored tissue paper strips, etc.)
12. FRICTION TESTING: wooden block, washers, paper clips, string, pushpins, materials to test such as sandpaper, marbles, straws
13. INERTIA CHALLENGES: coins, narrow-necked bottle, clay, heavy paper, glass, tray with sides
14. THE GREAT SLOW RACE: cardboard, marbles, construction materials, tape or pins, stopwatch

HEAT

1. HOT OR NOT?

The soup is too hot. The bath water is freezing. We are constantly commenting about the temperature. But some of the time you can't tell the difference between hot and cold. Here is an experiment to prove it.

Materials
Ice water, hot tap water, room-temperature water, three bowls (large enough to put your hands in), blindfold, towel,

Experiment
1. Set out three bowls and label them. Fill one with ice water, one with room-temperature water, and the third with tap water as hot as you can stand to put your hand in.
2. Ask a friend to rearrange the bowls without your looking. Put on the blindfold.
3. Have your friend put one of your hands in the hot water. Tell your friend how the water feels and have him or her record your answer.
4. Have your friend place your other hand in the cold water, leaving your first hand in the hot water.
5. After both hands have been immersed for about a minute, dry off the cold hand and have your friend place it in the room-temperature water. How does it feel?
6. Do the same with your other hand. Have your friend record your feeling.
7. Take your hands out of the water and have your friend put both of them into the warm water at the same time. Have him or her record your feeling. Remove the blindfold.
8. Reverse places and record your friend's sensations.

Ideas to Think About
1. How can the warm water be two different temperatures?
2. Did the water change temperature?
3. What do you think is happening?

What's Happening
Our skin is studded with nerves for sensing hot and cold. However, our temperature sensors aren't very good all by themselves—they're better at sensing temperature differences compared to something else. If you go wading in a cool stream, your feet will feel cold. If you wade in ice water for a moment and then wade in a cool stream, the cool stream will seem warm—in comparison.

Extension
Try the temperature experiment with family members or other friends. Compare the results.

ACTUAL TEMP	FEELS LIKE
HOT	
MED	
MED	
COLD	

2. HEAT DETECTIVE

Our body sensors are not very reliable instruments for sensing heat. You need a thermometer to get a good reading of just how hot or cold things are. Using a liquid crystal thermometer is an interesting way to find the hot spots and cold spots in your world.

Ideas to Think About
1. How do you tell the temperature? Where do you get the information?
2. How do you know what to wear each day?

THERMOMETER CARD

Materials
Liquid crystal thermometer card*

IF BAND IS TAN, CLOSER TO 70; IF BAND IS GREEN, IN THE MIDDLE; IF BAND IS BLUE, CLOSER TO 75.

Activity
Look at the thermometer card. What do you observe? What changes? What stays the same? What happens when you put one in light? in light and shadow? when you put your hand on it?

What's Happening
A liquid crystal thermometer is a new kind of thermometer that uses changes in light to show changes in temperature. Crystals, like cut diamonds, have the ability to bend light and break it into colors. Light passes through the liquid crystal material and shows up as a color. Heat causes the crystals to twist, making a change in the way they bend light.

To tell the temperature with a liquid crystal thermometer, read the lit-up band with the highest number. To tell where the temperature falls in that five-degree band, read the blue for the upper limit, green for the middle, and tan for the lower.

* Available from the Exploratorium store in San Francisco. To order, call 415-524-7400.

HEAT SURVEY

Materials
Liquid crystal thermometer cards

Survey
1. Take a temperature survey around the room. Find the hot spots and the cold spots.
2. Record your results with a map.

HEAT DETECTIVE
Find out the hot spots and cold spots in your home. Be sure not to put the thermometer cards in heated equipment like toaster ovens, although holding them near a heat source until they hit the top of the scale is okay. DO NOT HOLD THE CARDS NEAR OPEN FLAMES.

Materials
Liquid crystal thermometer cards

Activity
1. Begin by making a list or map predicting where you think the hot spots in your home will be.
2. Test your home with the thermometer cards.
3. List five hot spots at your house. List five cold spots.
4. Make a list of the sources of the hot spots.

3. BOTTLE THERMOMETER

Here is a simple thermometer that you can make from a pop bottle. You can use it to study the expanding and shrinking principles of all liquid temperature-telling devices.

Materials
Pop bottle, cork with a hole or plasticine clay, drinking straw, food coloring, water

Activity
1. Fill the bottle to the top with cool water.
2. Add food coloring to the water to make it a bright color.
3. Push the straw into the cork or clay.
4. Push the cork into the bottle. Make sure that it is in tight. The water level should touch the cork.
5. Seal the area around the straw with extra clay if needed.

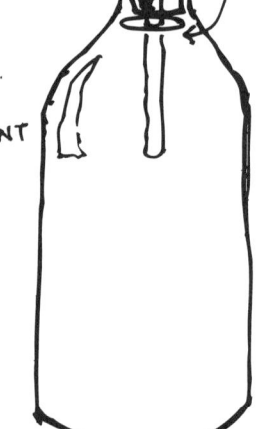

Ideas to Think About
1. You have made a simple thermometer. What do you think will happen when you put it in the sun? Draw your prediction. Test it. Record what happens.
2. What will happen if you put the bottle thermometer in ice water? What will happen to the water level? Record your prediction and try it.

Extension
How do you think you might get your bottle thermometer to tell the temperature in degrees? Calibrate your thermometer according to your decision. Mark the lower reading in ice water. Make an upper reading by putting the bottle in boiling water (do this slowly so it doesn't break). Take the daily temperature. What is wrong with using this method?

4. HOT ATOMS

The hotter something is, the faster the atoms in that thing are moving. You can actually see the result of atomic motion. All you need is hot and cold water and a bit of color to mark the action.

TEACHER DEMONSTRATION

Materials
Two clear bottles, ice water, very hot water, food coloring

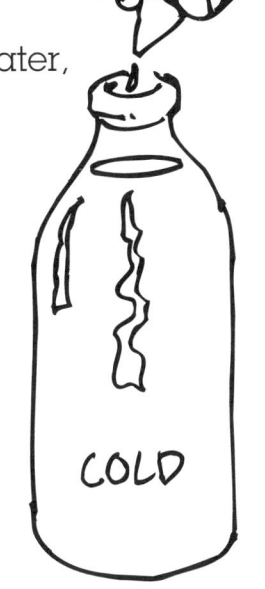

Demonstration
1. Fill one bottle with very hot water.
2. Fill the other with very cold water.
3. Wait until the water becomes still.
4. Tell the children to observe what happens in the hot and cold bottles. Add several drops of bright food coloring to each.
5. Record the results with a Venn diagram.

What's Happening
The molecules in the hot water are moving faster than those in the cold water. As they bump into each other, they bump the dye molecules and cause them to spread much more quickly. Because the molecules in the cold water are moving more slowly, the dye is bumped around and spreads at a slower rate.

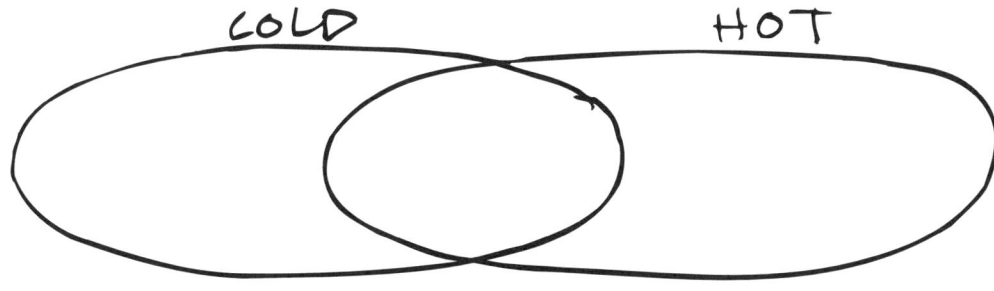

Table-Top Science: Intermediate ©1997 Monday Morning Books, Inc.

STUDENT EXPERIMENT

Materials
Clear cups, very hot water, ice water, room-temperature water, Kool-Aid powder, sugar, ice

Experiment
1. Set up three cups: one with hot water, the second with ice water, and the third with room-temperature water.
2. Predict which cup of water will spread the Kool-Aid color the fastest when you add it. Predict which cup will spread the Kool-Aid color the next fastest and the slowest.
3. Add a pinch of Kool-Aid powder to each cup.
4. Record what happens.
5. Pour all the experiments together, add sugar and ice, and drink the refreshment after you observe the results.

5. POPCORN BALLS

Add more heat to a thing and its atoms start getting excited. But then some interesting things begin to happen: solids melt into liquids and liquids vanish into the air as gas. The scientific term for this temperature event is phase change—but we often just call it cooking.

Ideas to Think About
What happens when you put heat under a solid? What happens when you take it away? What happens when you put heat under ice cream? paper? a coat hanger? bubble gum? a plastic cup? popcorn? sugar? Observe what happens to each ingredient in the following recipe. Identify whether each ingredient is a solid, liquid, or gas.

TEACHER DEMONSTRATION

Popcorn Balls (makes 10 small balls)

Ingredients
1/2 cup (125 grams) unpopped popcorn
2/3 cup (165 grams) sugar
1/2 cup (125 milliliters) water
2 1/2 tablespoons (13 milliliters) white corn syrup
dash of salt
1/3 teaspoon (2 milliliters) vinegar

Equipment
Popcorn maker, big pot with lid, measuring cup and spoons, candy thermometer, oil or margarine for greasing hands, stove or hot plate, spoon, towels

To Make the Popcorn
Cook the popcorn in an air popper, a microwave, or on the stove. Any ideas about why heating popcorn makes it pop? Do all corn kernels pop?

Table-Top Science: Intermediate ©1997 Monday Morning Books, Inc.

What's Happening
Corn kernels have a high water content. When heated, the water inside turns to gas. The atoms of trapped water vapor move so fast and with such force that they blow the sides out of the corn kernels with a pop! Only corn with a high water content will pop.

To Make the Syrup
1. Add all the ingredients except the popcorn to a large pot. Turn on the heat.
2. Stir until the sugar is melted.
3. Bring to a boil.
4. Cover and cook for about three minutes until steam washes down the sides.
5. Uncover and cook without stirring to hard crack stage.

STUDENT ACTIVITY

To Make the Popcorn Balls
1. Pour the syrup over the popcorn.
2. Stir until well coated.
3. Rub fingers with a dab of margarine so they become lightly oiled.
4. When the corn is cool enough to handle, take a handful of candied corn. Form it into a ball. Feel it harden. Continue making balls with the rest of the candied corn.
5. List all the phase changes that happened.

Science Book Page

RECORD PHASE CHANGES

Solids, liquid and gas are the 3 phases. Write the changes you saw, making a

RECORD PHASE CHANGES

Solids, liquid and gas are the 3 phases. Write the changes you saw, making a

6. INTERESTING DEGREES

Here on Earth the temperature is pretty steady. We forget that everything has a melting point and a boiling point if it is hot or cold enough. But how hot or cold is that? It is hard to get a sense of temperatures unless you compare them. Make a temperature scale and explore the amazing range of temperatures.

Ideas to Think About
You might start this activity by closing your eyes and imagining things: the gas in a helium balloon turning solid; a nail getting soft and melting like a candle; silver coins in your pocket turning to a runny liquid; a rose so cold and brittle that it can shatter like glass; a glass so hot it acts like jelly. All of these things can happen if the temperature changes.

Materials
Temperature cards, scissors, pushpins, paper, marker

Activity
1. Make a temperature scale and pin it up.
2. What temperatures do you already know? (You may know the melting and freezing points of water, the normal human body temperature, yesterday's temperature, etc.)
3. Cut out the temperature cards and choose one. Read what it says and pin it on the chart. Have several friends choose cards and pin them up.

300 million-400 million degrees C	middle of an atom bomb.
5,330 degrees C	surface of the sun
962 degrees C	silver melts
2,210 degrees C	silver boils
1,730 degrees C	molten lava
480 degrees C	Venus
-270 degrees C	outer space
-272 degrees C	helium freezes solid

Temperature Scale

1. Copy this page.

2. Cut out the strips at the right along the dotted lines.

3. Tape them together end to end. Make sure absolute zero is the first section in the strip.

4. Add more strips to the scale to reach at least 1500 degrees.

5. Hang the scale up on a wall.

Note: You might want to make your own larger and longer scale. The paper strips that come from adding machines work well.

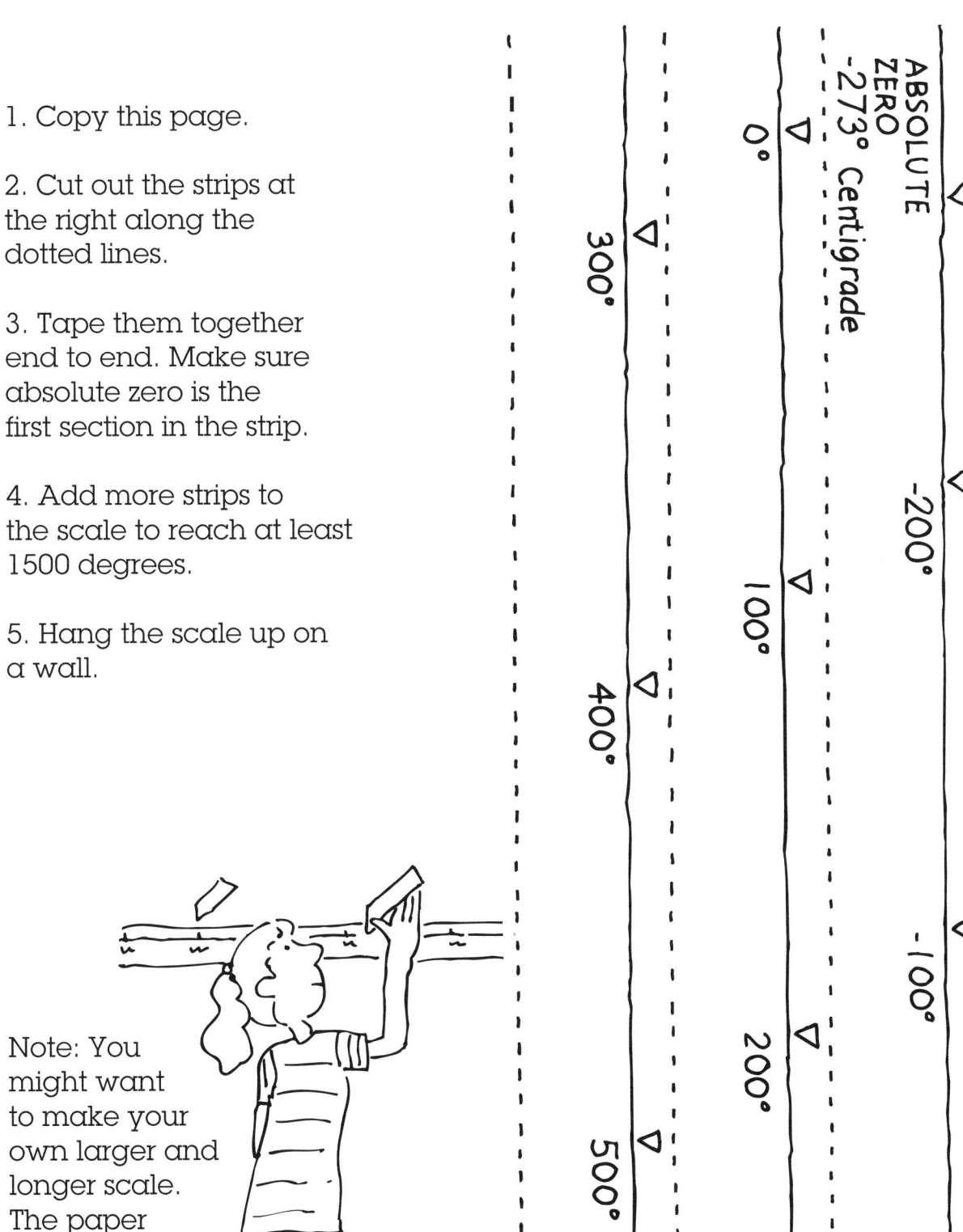

Temperature Cards

- 30° C — Butter Melts
- 44° C — Human Cells break down
- 20° C — Room temperature
- 0° C — Water freezes
- -1° C — Arctic sea water
- -183° C — Oxygen boils
- -270° C — Outer space
- -272° C — Helium freezes
- -273° C — Absolute zero (all atomic motion stops)

Temperature Cards

5,660° C   Sun's surface

4,200° C   Earth's core

2,530° C   Red star's surface

2,210° C   Silver boils

1,730° C   Molten lava

962° C   Silver melts

480° C   Venus's surface

100° C   Water boils

58° C   Earth (highest shade)

37° C   Human body

7. CONDUCTOR TESTS

Different materials have different properties. One of the important properties of a material is how it reacts to heat. Some materials melt at low temperatures, but some can absorb tremendous amounts of heat before they even begin to melt. Materials that allow heat to travel through them are called good conductors. Make some tests to discover some good and poor conductors.

Ideas to Think About
1. Why do cooking pots have rubber or wood handles?
2. Why is it colder to stand on tile on a bathroom floor than on a fluffy bath mat?

TEACHER DEMONSTRATION

Materials
Artist's wax, marbles, candles, matches, cardboard strips, strips of materials to test, such as copper, brass, glass, and wood

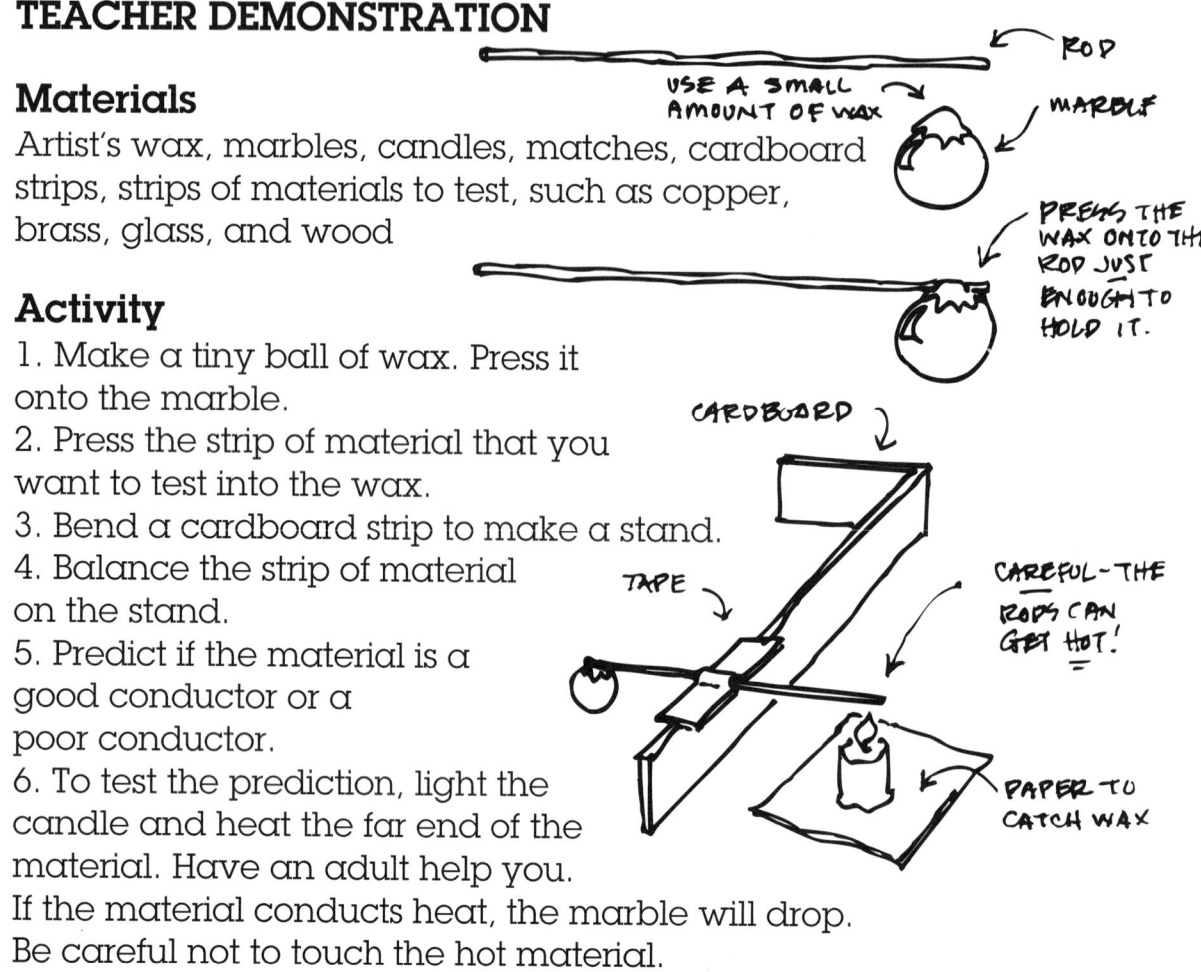

Activity
1. Make a tiny ball of wax. Press it onto the marble.
2. Press the strip of material that you want to test into the wax.
3. Bend a cardboard strip to make a stand.
4. Balance the strip of material on the stand.
5. Predict if the material is a good conductor or a poor conductor.
6. To test the prediction, light the candle and heat the far end of the material. Have an adult help you.
If the material conducts heat, the marble will drop. Be careful not to touch the hot material.
7. Record the results.
8. Test the other materials. Record all the results on a Venn diagram.

What's Happening

Heat moves from one place to another in different ways. When it moves through a solid object, it is called conduction. Some materials conduct heat well, some conduct heat poorly. Another name for a poor conductor is an insulator.

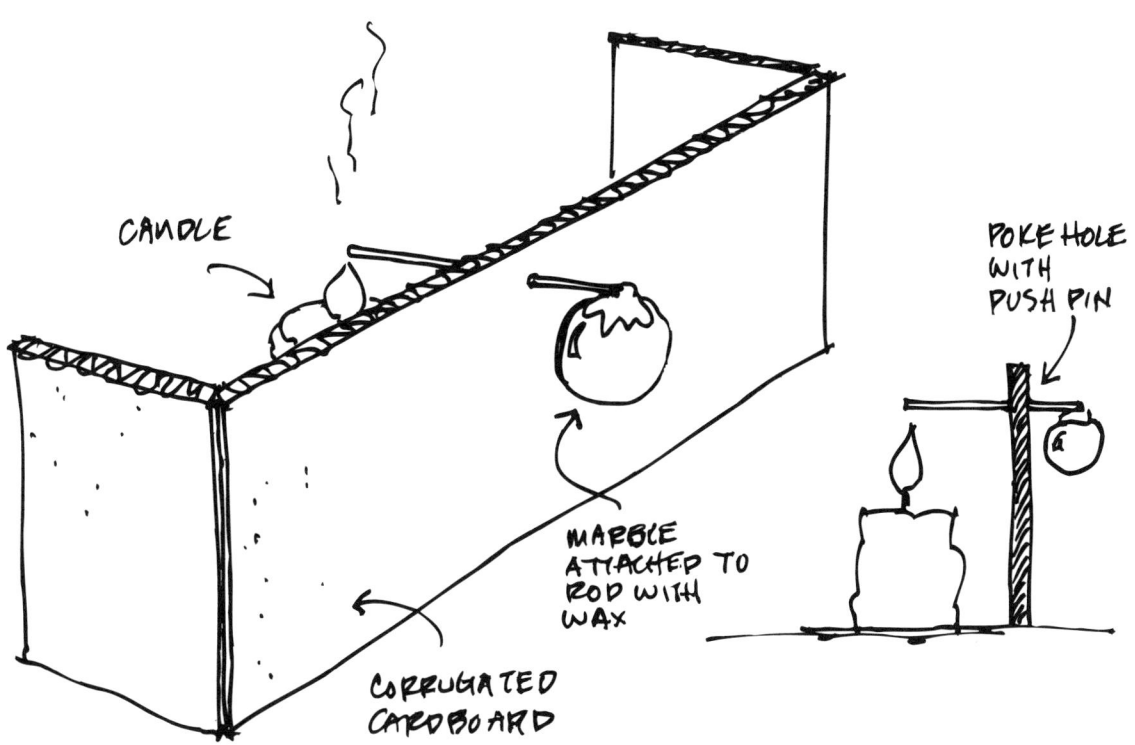

8. THE COOLEST KID

Who is the coolest kid in the room? Who is really hot? Take a temperature survey of everyone in the room and find out about the range of body temperatures.

Ideas to Think About
1. What does it mean when someone says you have a temperature? Is there ever a time when you don't have a temperature?
2. Do you know what your body temperature is? Why is it important?

Materials
Strip thermometers

Activity
1. Work with a friend. Each of you take a strip thermometer and try them out. Strip thermometers work best at room temperature away from strong light.
2. After a few minutes, write down your observations.
3. Put the strip on your friend's dry forehead just above the eyebrows. Hold the strip in place by the white ends.
4. Leave the strip in place for 15 seconds or until the color stops changing.
5. While holding the strip in place, read the temperature by looking at the last illuminated dot. If the dot is green, the temperature is the number next to the dot. If the dot is tan, the temperature is one degree less than the number next to the dot. If the dot is blue, the temperature is one degree more than the number next to the dot.
6. Record your friend's temperature on a paper square. Put his or her name on the back.
7. Change places and let your friend find out your temperature. Write down the result.

8. If several pairs of children have found each other's temperatures, graph the results by putting each child's temperature square on the graph. Who is the "coolest" kid in the room? the "hottest?" Which kids are "average?"

What's Happening

The cells in our bodies change food into energy, or metabolize it, to fuel all our bodies' activities. A byproduct of all that activity is heat. You can tell how fast (or hard) your body is working by measuring the heat it gives off. This heat is what we call a temperature. When people say you have a temperature, they mean you have a higher than average temperature, or a fever. But every person does not have the same average temperature. One person's fever may be the average or normal temperature for another person. It is important to know what normal is for you.

Extension

What is the average temperature of all the children tested?

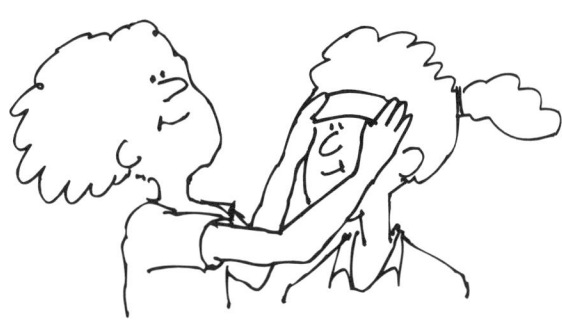

→ Find the average:

9. DAILY DEGREES

Do you think you are a one-temperature person? Or do you think your body temperature changes during the day? Is there anything you can do to make your temperature change?

HIGH SPOTS AND LOW SPOTS

Materials
Strip thermometers

Experiment
1. Make a prediction about whether you think your temperature changes during the day.
2. Work with a partner and track your temperatures during the day. Take your temperatures after sitting still, after eating, after hard exercise, and after other activities you decide on.
3. Record your findings.
4. Make a graph of the high spots and low spots.

What's Happening
Bodies show short-term temperature changes according to the activities they are doing. Eating and exercising generally have the most effect.

DAILY RHYTHMS

Materials
Strip thermometers

Experiment
1. Predict whether you think there is a pattern to your temperature changes.
2. Work with a partner and track your temperatures during the day.
3. Record your findings.
4. Make a graph of the high spots and low spots.

What's Happening
If you could accurately track your temperature hourly over a 24-hour period, you might begin to see a pattern. Humans generally show a 24-hour pattern of rising and falling body activity. What is important to know is that everybody can expect to have times when they feel strong and alert and times when they feel quiet and sleepy. If you know your body you can begin to take advantage of its natural patterns or biorhythms.

Amazing Facts
1. The typical range of body temperatures is:
   Resting: 97.2 to 99.2 degrees F (36.2 to 37.3 degrees C)
   During physical activity: 100 degrees F (37.7 degrees C)
   During illness: 102 to 104 degrees F (38.8 to 40 degrees C)
2. A byproduct of metabolism is heat. The faster and harder the body works, the more heat it produces.
3. During heavy exercise, the body can pump up its metabolic rate 150 to 200 times its resting level for short spurts.
4. The slowest metabolic rate takes place during sleep, the fastest during hard exercise.
5. Fever is a sign the body is working hard to fight off infection.
6. When body temperature rises 4 degrees, the body is changing food to energy about 28 times faster than normal.

10. YOUR HOT SPOTS

Does your body have hot spots? Make a bet, then use a temperature strip to test your theory.

Ideas to Think About
Cold feet? Freezing fingers? Remember how putting your hands into cold and hot water in the "Hot or Not?" activity proved that your ability to sense temperatures can be confused? Are parts of your body really colder than others? Or is it your imagination? What do you think? What are your reasons for thinking this?

Materials
Strip thermometers

Experiment
1. Predict whether or not you have hot spots. Write down your prediction. (If you think you have hot spots, predict where they might be.)
2. Hold the temperature strip on various parts of your skin. Try places like your hands, your forehead, and your tummy.
3. Read and record the results.
4. Where is your hottest spot? Have some friends do the experiment and see if their hot spots are the same as yours.

What's Happening

Your extremities—your hands, feet, and face—can be much colder (at least on the surface) than the rest of your body. The clothes on the parts of your body that you keep covered trap the heat next to your body. These thermos bottle-like pockets of air keep your core warmer than usually uncovered body parts such as hands and face. Keeping your body core heat up is important. When it drops significantly you are in trouble and could die from hypothermia.

Extension

Animals have come up with all sorts of ways to keep warm as well as cool. Brainstorm the ways creatures in the natural world keep their body temperatures just right.

11. COOLING SWEAT

Sweating is really cool! Prove it yourself with this plastic mitten experiment. Then learn about another cool liquid.

A PLASTIC MITTEN AND EVAPORATION

Materials
Plastic bags, rubber bands

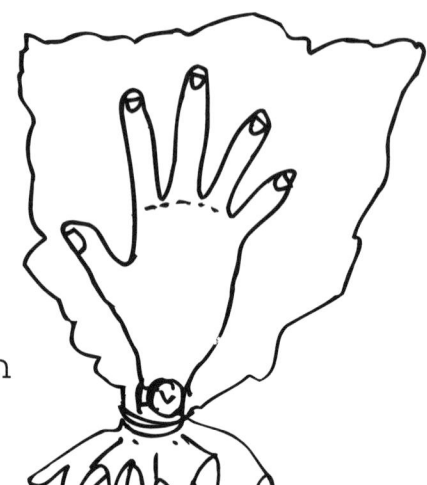

Experiment
1. Put a plastic bag over one hand.
2. Secure it at the wrist with a rubber band.
3. Predict what the hand with the plastic mitten will feel like after five minutes.
4. Record your prediction.
5. Remove the bag after five minutes.
6. Blow on both hands. Record your observations.

Ideas to Think About
Why is it foggy in the bag? Where does the damp come from? What is it doing? Why is it cool when you remove the bag?

What's Happening
Everyone knows that sweat keeps you cool. But this is not exactly true. It is the drying up or evaporating of sweat that keeps you cool. When a substance evaporates (changes from a liquid to a gas), there is a temperature drop. Sweating is the body's way of taking advantage of this fact. Glands in the skin ooze water onto the skin. When the water evaporates into the air, the temperature on the skin drops and the body cools. The faster the liquid evaporates, the cooler it feels.

RUBBING ALCOHOL AND EVAPORATION

How does your head feel with wet hair? How does your skin feel when you're standing around wet after a swim? What if the wind is blowing? Water has the ability to cool you off by evaporating on your skin. But what about another liquid like salad oil? Do you think that would have the same cooling power as water? How about rubbing alcohol?

Materials
Cotton balls, rubbing alcohol, cups, water, blindfold

Experiment
1. Blindfold a friend.
2. Pour some water in a cup. Pour some rubbing alcohol in another cup.
3. Dip one cotton ball in the alcohol. Dip another in the water.
4. Dab the fingertips of one of your friend's hands with alcohol. Dab the other with water.
5. Which does he or she think feels cooler?
6. Record your results.
7. Change places and have your friend dab your fingers with water and rubbing alcohol. Record the results.
8. Dab an area on a table top with water and another with rubbing alcohol. Watch the rate of evaporation.
9. Do you see any difference between the rate of evaporation of water and that of rubbing alcohol? Do you think the rate of evaporation has anything to do with the cooling power?

Ideas to Think About
Why does it feel cool in a draft? Why use a fan in hot weather? Why do cowboys pour water in their hats on a hot day? Why do elephants spray themselves with water? Why do wet socks make cold feet?

12. IS HOT PINK HOT?

If you want to keep warm, should you wear hot pink? On a summer day should you wear cool blue? Here is a test to find out if colors have any effect on heat.

Materials
Thermometer, colored construction paper (plus black and white), tape or staples, sunlight, scissors

Experiment
1. Cut out jackets of colored paper.
2. Staple the sides shut.
3. Are some colors cooler than others? Make your prediction.
4. Slide the thermometer into one of the colored paper jackets.
5. Record the temperature.
6. Put the thermometer into the other colored jackets. Record the temperatures.
7. Put the thermometer in one jacket in direct sunlight.
8. Record the temperature after five minutes. Do the same with the other jackets.
9. Summarize the results on a graph. Record the colors and their temperatures.

Ideas to Think About
Based on the results, which color would you choose to wear on a hot sunny day? What color would keep you warmest?

What's Happening

Hot objects like a fire or the sun give off, or radiate, invisible infrared rays of energy. These rays can travel across space or through the air. When these rays hit an object, the energy is absorbed and the thing they hit heats up. You've been able to experience this if you've ever stood in front of a fireplace or tried to avoid a worse sunburn. As you've discovered in this experiment, light colors reflect radiant heat while dark colors absorb radiant heat. You can read this difference on the thermometer.

More to Explore

For a more complete graph of the color experiment, record the temperature for each color every minute for five minutes. Record it again every minute for five minutes after you take each jacket out of the sun. Compare the temperature pictures. Discuss what the different profiles mean.

Heat Glossary

calibrate: mark the graduations or degrees (of a thermometer).
Celsius: the temperature scale which divides the interval between the melting and freezing point of water into 100 degrees. This temperature scale is used by scientists and is also called Centigrade.
conductor: heat travels through some materials very well, and poorly through other materials. (A metal spoon dipped in hot water heats up quickly, a wooden spoon heats up only a bit. Metal is a good conductor, wood is a poor conductor of heat.)
evaporation: changing from a solid or liquid state into a gas.
Fahrenheit: this temperature scale takes the freezing point of water as the low and human body temperature as the high. It divides the interval between these into 96 degrees. In Fahrenheit water freezes at 32 degrees and boils at 212 degrees. This scale was invented by Gabriel D. Fahrenheit.
gas: one of the three states of matter. Gases take the shape of the container they are in, and generally can't be seen or felt. Steam is water in the gas state.
insulator: another name for a poor conductor of heat. Wood, rubber, and fiberfill are materials used as insulators.
liquid: one of the three states of matter. Liquids flow into any shape. Water is a liquid.
metabolism: name for the cellular activity in which food is changed into energy to fuel the body's functions. A by-product of cell activity is heat.
molecule: a group of tiny particles (atoms) that makes up a substance.
states of matter: every substance given the right conditions can be a solid, liquid, or gas. Molecules in a solid are densely packed; in a liquid molecules are less densely packed; in a gas they are loosely connected. The molecules that make up a gas move faster than either a liquid or a solid.
solid: one of the three states of matter. Solids are rigid, and tend to keep their shape. Ice is a solid.
vapor: gas.

Cells

HELPFUL HINTS

Using the Microscope

It takes some practice to get used to using a high-power microscope. Go slow and start with easy specimens until you get the feel of it.

• Beginners are convinced they can see more with higher power. The opposite is usually true. Lower powers let in more light, giving a brighter image. Lower powers also allow more of a specimen to be seen so you can find your way around the thing you're viewing.
• Expert microscope users keep both eyes open when using the microscope to prevent strain. This may be too hard for you. You may find it easier to look with one eye and cup your fingers over the other eye to block out the distracting view.
• If you see long hairy things when you look through the scope, don't panic. If they blink when you do, you know they are your eyelashes.
• Sometimes there seems to be floating stuff on a slide. Often these squiggles are floating in your own eye. Just ignore them. With a little practice, you won't notice them anymore.
• Light is important. Getting the light adjusted is half the battle:
1. Don't use direct sunlight. This could hurt your eyes. Instead, catch the light bounced off a bright, white wall or work next to a window.
2. Keep your hand out of the way of the light source when you adjust a slide. It is easy to block the mirror while peering through the eyepiece, and you'll get frustrated when everything suddenly goes black.
3. Battery-powered light works better in dim surroundings. That's because your eye isn't overpowered by a bright background.
4. High-power scopes have a diaphragm with holes that open

and shut to adjust the amount of light. Admitting too much light on transparent specimens can make them too washed out to see. Shut down the light. Try using the blue filter or the red one. Experiment to see what works best.

5. Sometimes it helps to move the scope so that more light comes across the slide from the top or the side. Doing this lets you catch some interesting prism effects with insect wings, crystals, and fish scales.

6. Moving the slide around lets you scout out the area that provides the best viewing. Remember that if you push the slide to the right it will appear to travel left (the optics of the scope reverse the motion).

• Don't expect what you see through the microscope to look like textbook pictures. What you see will usually be dimmer and fuzzier. Pictures in textbooks are made by professionals using the very best equipment and are often retouched in the printing process.

• Comparing what you see to illustrations of cells in books can also be misleading. Artists draw what is there, but they also leave out a lot of the fuzzy, out-of-focus parts. A cell you see through the scope will never look like an artist's drawing. The nucleus will never be as shiny and bright, the walls will not be in as sharp focus, and all those neat dots of cytoplasm will look more like oatmeal.

Preparing Slides

• Cut the thinnest specimens possible. Light must be able to pass through them for you to see anything. Also, thin sections allow you to look at one or two layers of cells rather than trying to observe a large mass.
• Make your sample a thin wedge shape that tapers out. This will make the outer edge paper thin for the best viewing.
• Cover slips are especially handy for wet slides because they help hold the specimen in position and keep everything flat. They also keep specimens from drying out and protect the lens from getting contaminated with liquid.
• Try to keep air bubbles from being trapped when you put on the cover slip (air bubbles appear as dark rings or circles). The best way to keep bubbles out is to put one edge of the slip in the liquid first and then lower the rest of it. With practice you'll get better at making wet slides with few bubbles.

1. LOW-POWER MAGNIFIERS

Simple, low-power magnifiers are fun to use for a couple of reasons. They are easy to use because the focusing is fixed and they don't need so much light. Also, it's easier to find your way around. There are plenty of fascinating discoveries to be made at lower powers. These magnifiers are finer and more powerful lenses than the ones used by early scientists such as Galileo.

Ideas to Think About

There are several kinds of low-power magnifiers that work well.

One is called a loupe, and it is an excellent 8 to 10 power magnifier. It is handy for trapping crawling things, and available from professional photo stores.

Another magnifier is called an illuminated microscope. These 30-power pocket scopes need batteries, and are portable and tough.

Using the Magnifier

1. Meet the magnifier. Set it down on a flat, stable surface where there is light and room to work.
2. Experiment with how to get the best focus. Try moving your eye closer to and farther from the lens.
3. Many lenses are plastic and easily scratched. Find out how to care for the lens.

Experiment
Start out using the magnifier to view something that won't wiggle. Samples of letters from magazines or color swatches will give you a good appreciation of scale.

Materials
Magazines, cardboard templates, pens, scissors, magnifier

Activity
1. Find a letter from a black and white page, or a color swatch. Put down the template. Trace a "slide" on the printed page.
2. Cut out the "slide."
3. Use the magnifier to view the slide.
4. Adjust the light to see if it improves your view. What do you see?
5. Make two drawings:
    - One with no magnification
    - One under the scope
6. Write what changed.

More to Explore
You will find that colored photos break down into wonderful dot patterns. Predict what color dots you will find in the green, blue, and brown areas of a photo. Then use the scope to find out if your prediction was true.

2. HOW BIG?

How big is big? For that matter, how small is small? Thirty-power magnification may not sound like much magnification. But ask the children to imagine that they are suddenly twice as big as they are now. How about 10 times bigger? Then have them do this activity that lets them explore the idea of scale.

Materials
Bee puzzle pieces, envelopes, scissors

TEACHER PREPARATION
1. Reproduce the puzzle pieces, one sheet at each magnification for each group of four to six children.
2. Cut the pieces apart.
3. Put each set of pieces into a separate envelope.
4. Distribute one set of pieces at each magnification to each group of children.

STUDENT EXPERIMENT

Materials
One set of puzzle pieces at each of four different magnifications, large sheets of drawing paper, markers

Activity
1. Work in a group. Take out the puzzle pieces from each envelope. Put together the four different puzzles.
2. Study the finished puzzles. Decide which puzzle shows 2X magnification, 3X magnification, 5X magnification, and 10X magnification.

Ideas to Think About
1. How much bigger is the biggest bee than the second biggest? the second biggest than the smallest?
2. What would the bee look like if it was 30 times bigger than the smallest bee? Draw what it would look like.

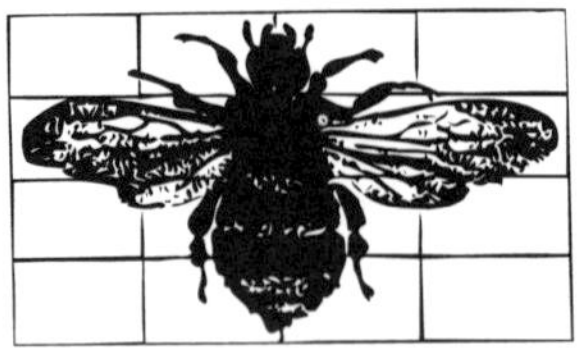

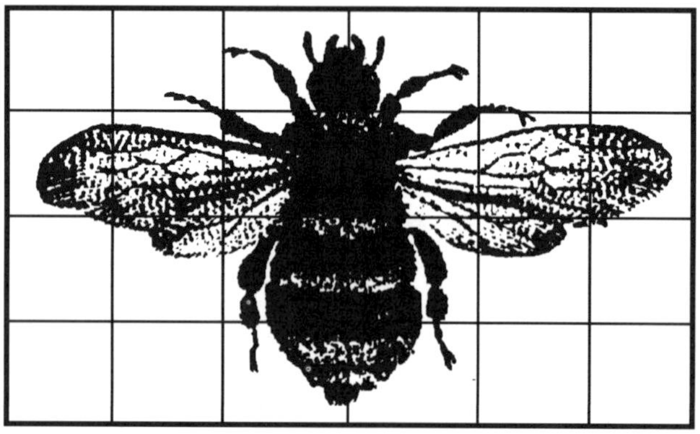

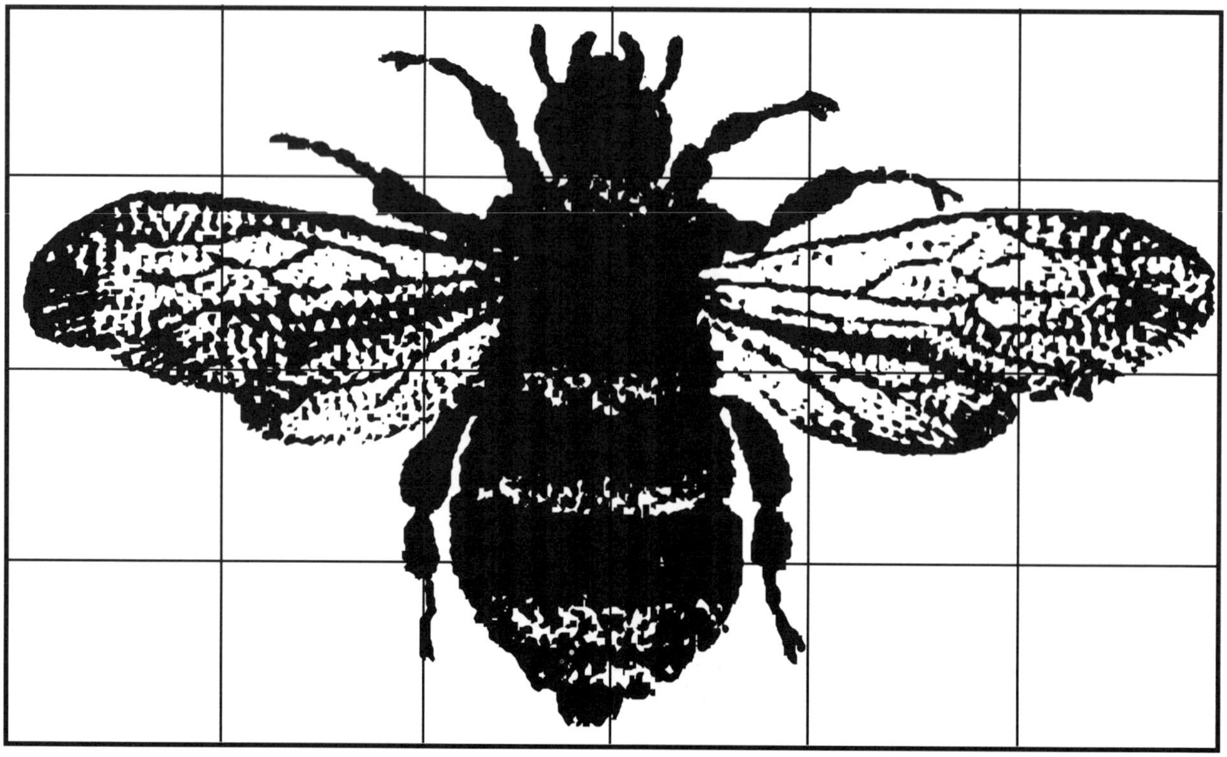

45

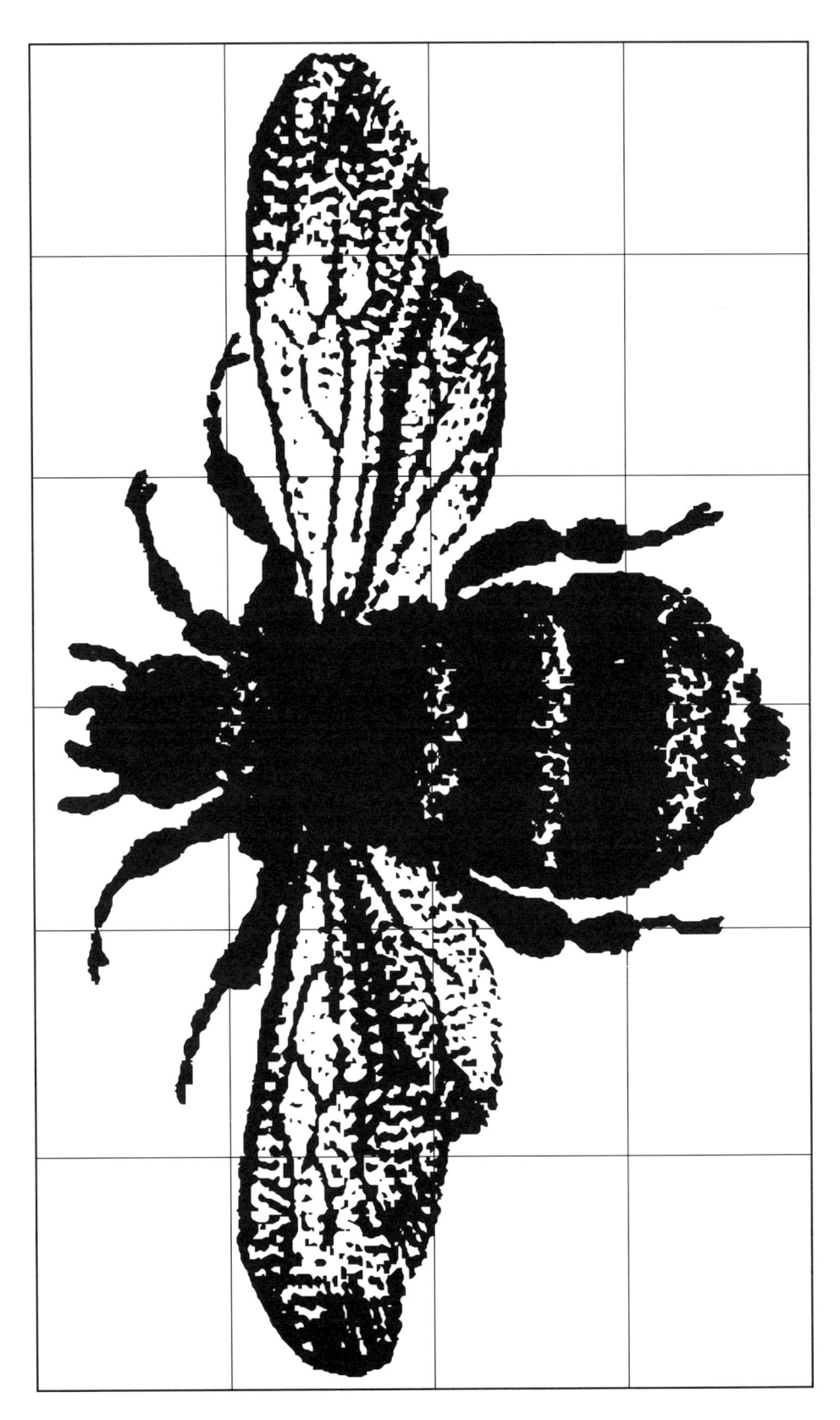

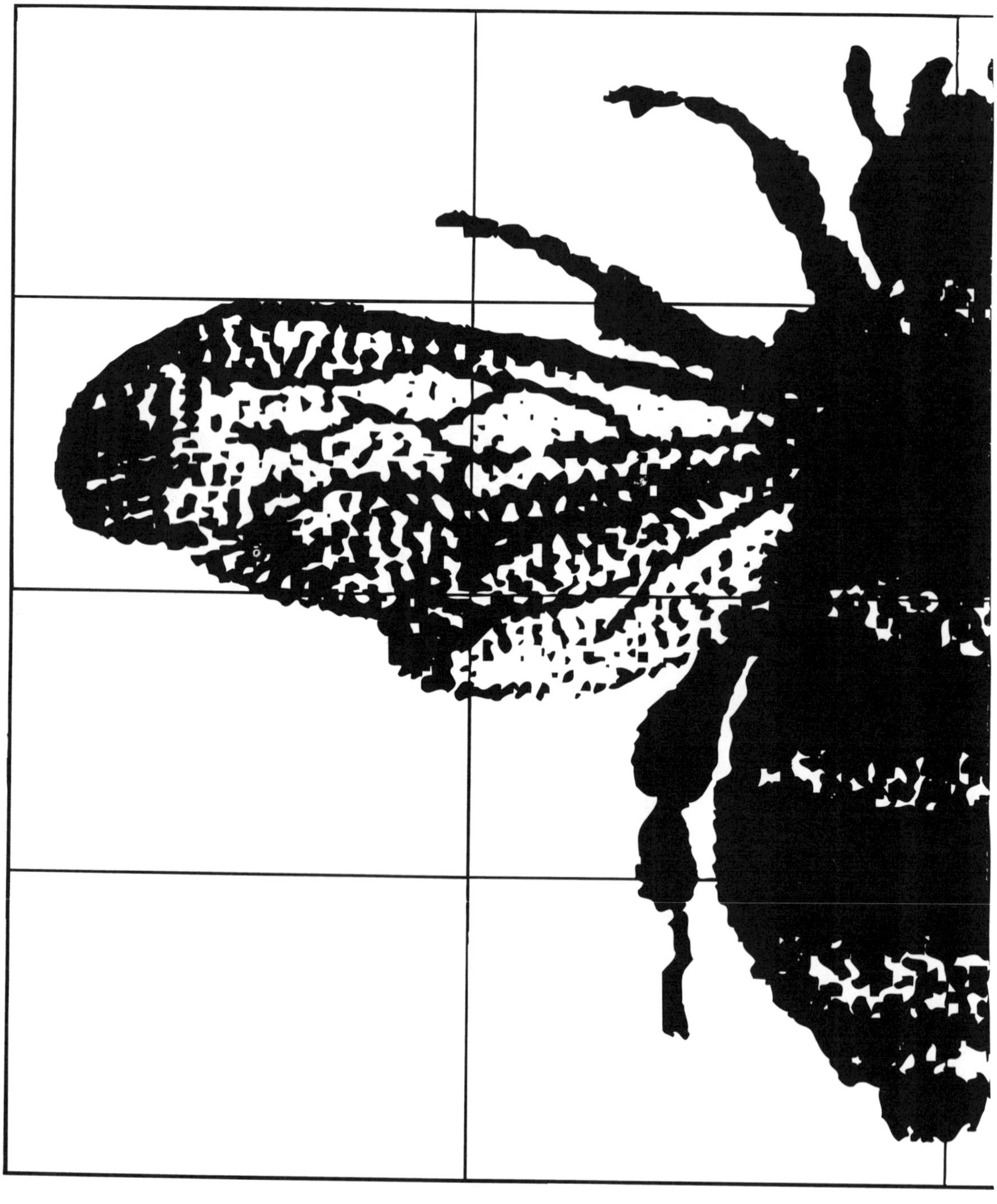

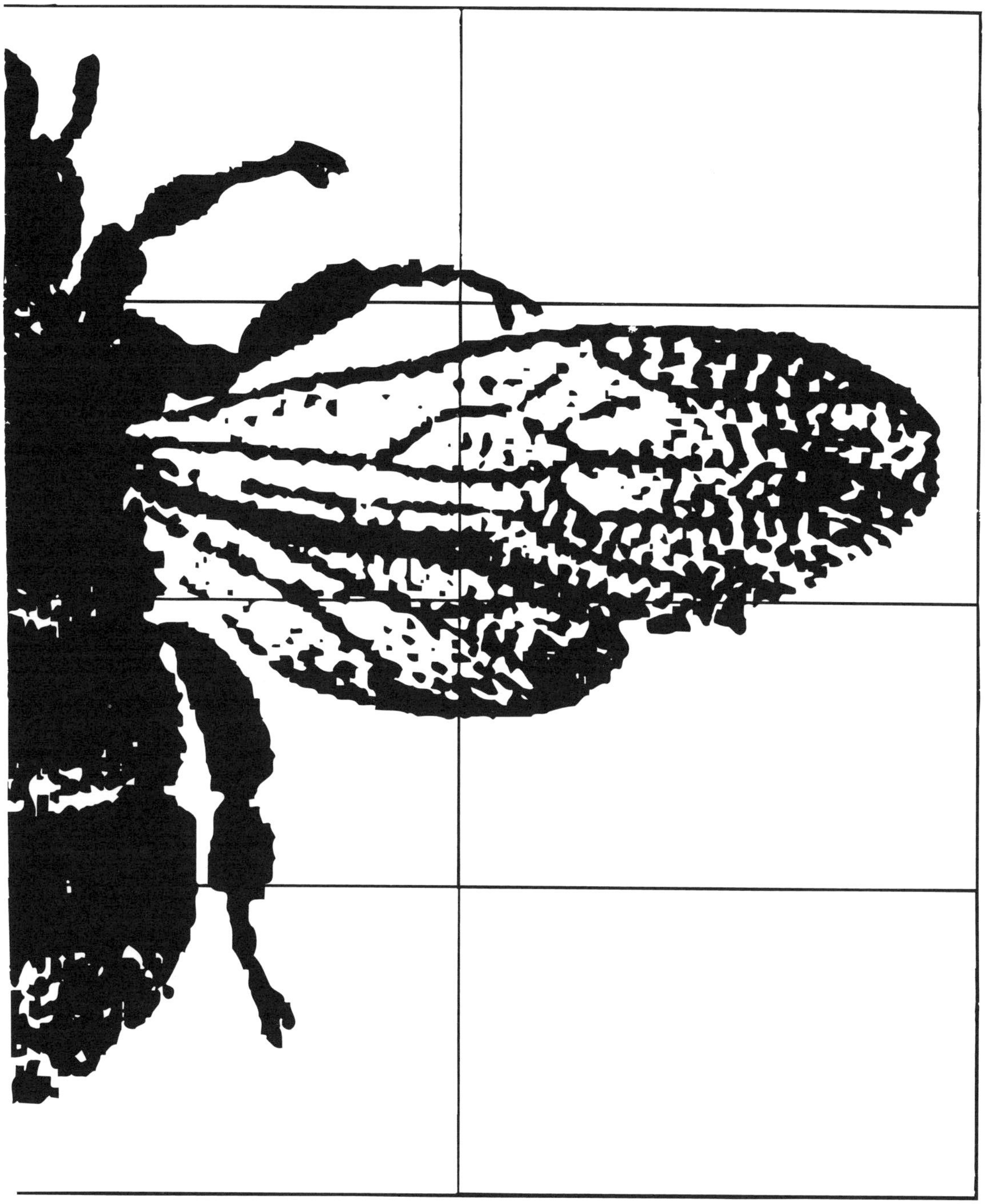

3. HIGH-POWER SCOPE

Meet your high-power scope. It has higher magnification, a handy artificial light, and other adjustments, but it is trickier to use. Go slowly. Expect some frustration until you and your students get the hang of it.

Microscope Cautions
- Always carry the scope by the arm.
- Don't use direct sunbeams. They can damage the eye.
- Clean the lenses with lens paper. Take care not to scratch lenses.
- Focus up, never down. This prevents jamming the lens into the slide.
- Some scopes have a built-in light. Turn it on by flipping the mirror. Make sure the mirror side is up when you're finished so you don't run down the batteries.

TEACHER DEMONSTRATION

Use this basic procedure with any higher-power scope.
1. Angle the mirror away from you. Face the mirror toward the light.
2. Remove the lens cap if it is on. Turn the eyepiece far to the right. (This adjusts it for lower power.)
3. Look through the lens. Angle the mirror so the field is bright as possible.
4. Center the specimen over the hole on the stage.
5. Start with low power. Low is easiest to use because there is the most light and more of the specimen to be seen.
6. Turn the focus knob so the lens is as close to the stage as possible. Focus up, slowly. Keep looking while you turn. The image will pop into focus.

Note: Alternate turning the eyepiece and the focus knob so you don't lose the focus.

STUDENT EXPERIMENT

1. Use the magazine slides from the first activity.
2. View them at the lowest power, then at the next highest.
3. Make drawings at all magnifications.

Hint: This kind of specimen works much better with bright light shining on top of it. (You can even use direct sun here.)

Suggestion

Work in teams with two students to a scope. It may work well for each team to use a low-power and a high-power scope. That way each team will have a less magnified view for comparison, and there will be less waiting because both students can record.

Meet a High-Power Scope

Every microscope model is slightly different, but all have similar parts. Can you find these parts on the scope you are using?

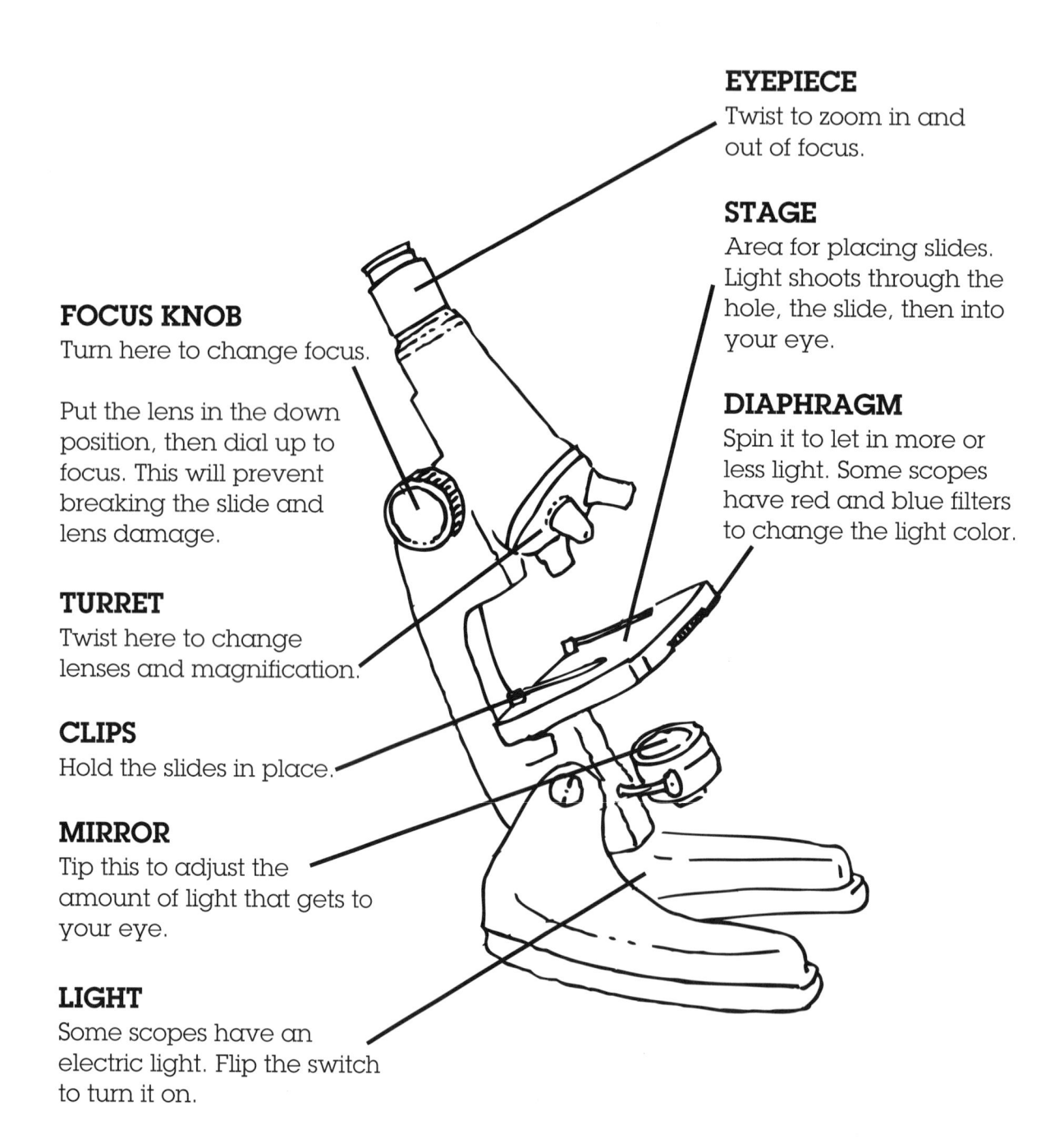

EYEPIECE
Twist to zoom in and out of focus.

STAGE
Area for placing slides. Light shoots through the hole, the slide, then into your eye.

DIAPHRAGM
Spin it to let in more or less light. Some scopes have red and blue filters to change the light color.

FOCUS KNOB
Turn here to change focus.

Put the lens in the down position, then dial up to focus. This will prevent breaking the slide and lens damage.

TURRET
Twist here to change lenses and magnification.

CLIPS
Hold the slides in place.

MIRROR
Tip this to adjust the amount of light that gets to your eye.

LIGHT
Some scopes have an electric light. Flip the switch to turn it on.

4. CORK CELLS

Look into a cork to see its structure.

Materials
High-power microscope, cork (one from an old wine bottle is fine), sharp razor blade, eyedropper, water, slide, cover slip, paper, markers

Teacher Preparation
1. Begin by preparing the slide:
• Cut several very thin slivers of cork.
• Place one on the slide.
• Add a drop of water and a cover slip.
2. Have students make drawings of the cork cell structure at high and low power.

What to Look For
Look for a lacy edge on the outer part of the cork. This is a network of cell walls. The cells line up like bricks.

What You Won't See
You won't see any protoplasm (living tissue) in the cells because they are dead. The cork, however, was once part of the living bark of a tree.

Ideas to Think About
Why do you think cork floats? Hint: The cells that are empty of protoplasm are filled with air. Can you guess why cork compresses so easily?

Amazing Facts
Cells got their name because the first person who looked at cork under a microscope, Robert Hooke, thought that the pattern he saw looked like a bunch of tiny rooms. Monasteries of the time were buildings with lots of tiny rooms for the people who lived there. The tiny rooms were called cells. Robert Hooke named the little boxes he saw under the microscope cells, and the name has stuck.

5. ONION SKIN

You can look into living skin and see the cell structure of a plant. Onion skin is a perfect material for this because it is very thin and allows light through. It is also fairly easy to handle.

TEACHER DEMONSTRATION

Materials
High-power microscope, slides, cover slip, white or yellow onion, mat knife, iodine, eyedropper

To Prepare the Slide
1. Cut the onion into half-inch sections.
2. Pull one of the sections apart to get one layer.
3. The layer has a smooth dry side and a wetter inner side. Cut a square from the skin on the inner side.
4. Pick up a corner of the skin. Carefully pull it away.
5. Lay it on the slide. Stretch it flat.
6. Cover the skin with a drop of the iodine stain. (If the stain won't take, turn the skin over.)
7. Put on the cover slip. Try not to get air bubbles.

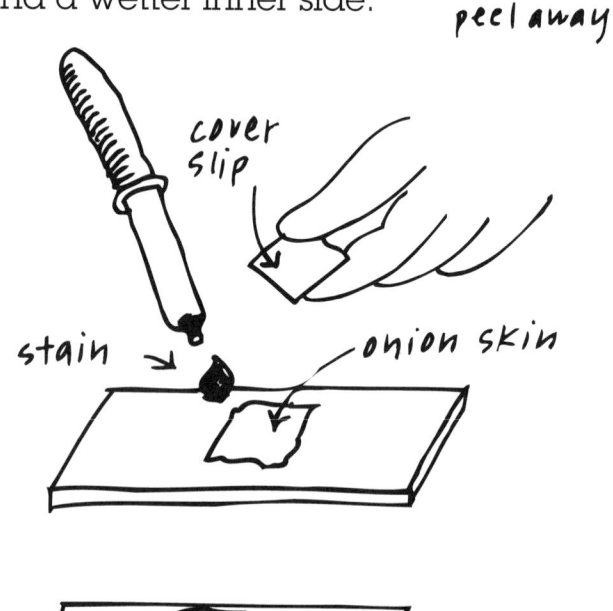

STUDENT EXPERIMENT

Materials
High-power microscope, slides, cover slip, white or yellow onion, mat knife, iodine, eyedropper, paper, markers

Activity
Prepare a slide the way you saw it done in the demonstration.

To View the Slide
1. Adjust the light source so the field is bright.
2. Start with the lowest power.
3. Adjust the focus so the lens is as close to the stage as possible. Focus up, slowly.
4. Make a drawing at high and low power.
5. If possible, also work with a simple scope for a different view.

What to Look For
Move the slide around. Notice the variety of cell shapes. Dark areas are often air bubbles. In a plant, the cells that manufacture food look different than the cells that transport food and water. Plant cells tend to have thick walls. Look for:

cells: boxy shapes, each a little different
cell walls: the thick parts that separate the cells from each other
nucleus: the dark blob in each cell
cytoplasm: the liquid part that fills each cell
chloroplast: the food-making center in a plant cell's cytoplasm that contains chlorophyll and gives the plant its green color

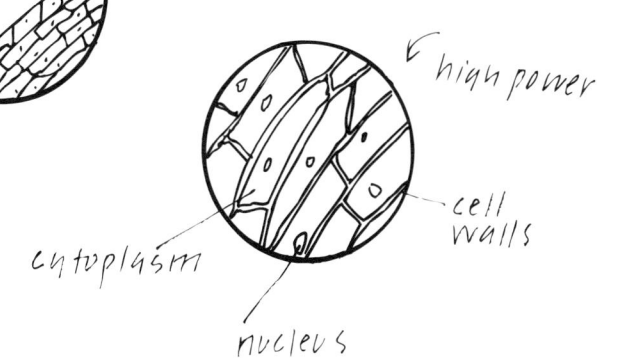

6. ELODEA

Elodea is a plant that you find in fishbowls and in ponds. Its leaves are only two cells thick, which makes it great for viewing with a microscope. Inside Elodea is the secret of green plants. Can you find it?

Materials
High-power microscope, slides, cover slips, eyedropper, water, Elodea leaves (available from a fish store; Elodea also goes by the name of Anacharis)

To Prepare the Slide
1. Pull off a single Elodea leaf.
2. Place it on the slide.
3. Add a drop of water.
4. Cover with a cover slip.

What to Look For
Green plants can turn light into food. The chlorophyll inside a cell is the material that performs this magic. Look for:

chloroplasts: green bodies in a cell that turn light into food
cytoplasm: the clear jelly that fills a cell

If conditions are right you can watch the cytoplasm inside an Elodea leaf move. If the cytoplasm is not streaming, warming the slide in the sun or in the palm of your hand for a few minutes might get it started. Leaves at the tip of the plant are most active.

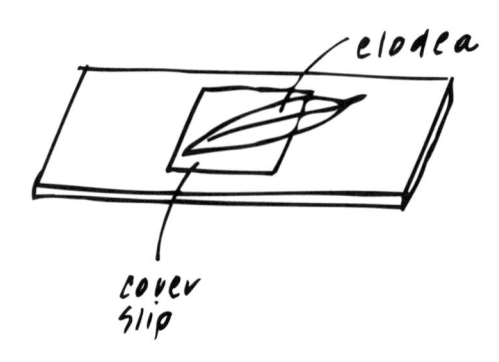

7. EEK! CHEEK CELLS

Take a look at some of your own cells. You'll be amazed at how many cells your skin constantly throws away. You are constantly making new skin cells. The old ones grow out and drop off. Every day your skin sloughs off millions of cells.

Materials
High-power microscope, slides, cover slip, toothpick or tongue depressor, iodine, eyedropper, needle

To Prepare the Slide
1. Scrape the inside of your cheek with a toothpick or tongue depressor.
2. Wipe the collected goo on the middle of a slide (with just one swipe you'll collect hundreds of cells!). Smear the material across the slide.
3. Add a drop of iodine stain.
4. Cover with a cover slip.

To View the Slide
1. Find an area on the slide where the cells are spread out. Cheek cells are transparent, so too much light will make them hard to see. At low power the cells will look like dandruff. At higher power you will see cells floating on top of each other.
2. Press the slide cover with the needle. You will see the cells float by. Focus up and down.
3. Find a cell that you like and view it at higher powers.
4. Make a drawing. Label the parts.

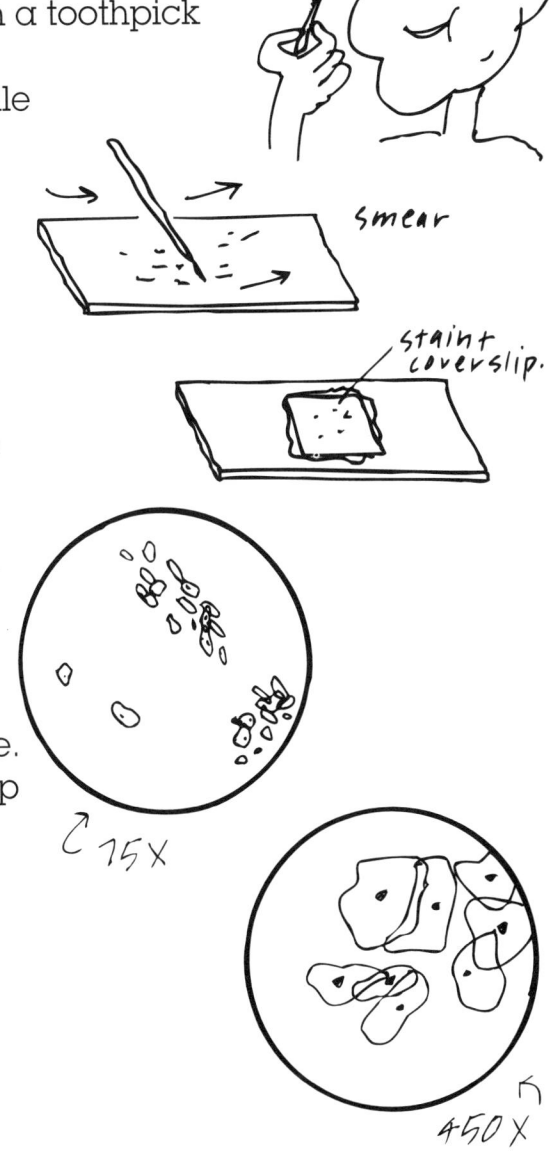

What to Look For

the lack of a cell wall: animal cells don't have thick cell walls, but instead have membranes; they also don't have as many vacuoles (food storage areas) as plant cells, but this is OK because animals eat constantly and don't make their own food

the lack of chloroplasts: animal cells don't contain any green food-making bodies

nucleus: the dark blob in each cell

the round cell shape: scraping distorts cells, but those in the best condition will still have a roundish shape

More to Explore

Compare the cells in your skin to those in onion skin.

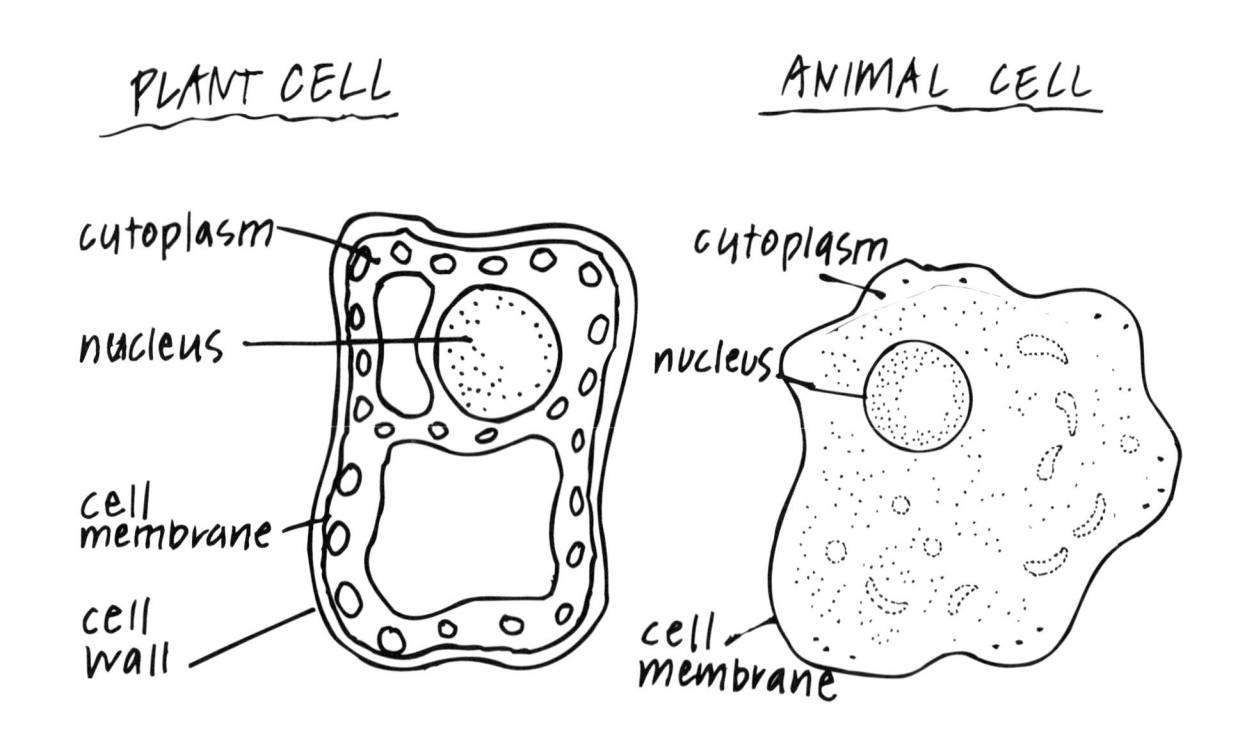

PLANT CELL — cytoplasm, nucleus, cell membrane, cell wall

ANIMAL CELL — cytoplasm, nucleus, cell membrane

8. ONE-CELLED ANIMALS

Most animals and plants are made up of vast colonies of billions of cells. But some animals and plants are only one cell big. Chances are you have never met one of these little creatures. A drop of pond water can reveal a whole world if you know how to look for it.

Materials

High-power microscope, slides, cover slips, eyedropper, pond water or sea water and plants (Note: You need to use water that is rich with organisms. Stagnant pools of fresh water are good places to look. Protected pools of sea water or sea water near pilings or docks are also good sources. You can also collect water from fishponds or fish tanks. Whichever type of water you collect, fill a large jar with it. Include mossy plants and a bit of soil if you can.)

To Prepare the Slide

1. Place a piece of moss on the slide. Use the thinnest sample you can find. The tangle of fibers tends to keep creatures stuck to them and to confine the fast-traveling ones so that you can see them.
2. Pull the moss sample apart to open it up.
3. Put a drop of water on the moss.
4. Put on the cover slip.
5. Keep the slide unclipped so that you can move it around and search for critters. Also keep the stage flat so that the water doesn't drip.

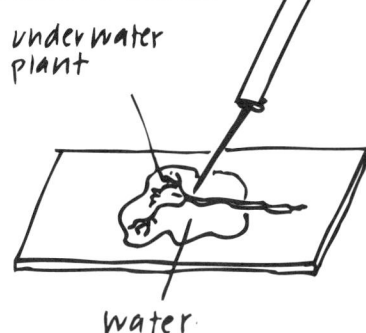

What to Look For

This is a hunting activity. Move the slide around and look for critters. They will probably be in the web of plant fibers. Notice the plant fibers' cell structure. Also notice the movement of little football-like creatures that look like they're playing bumper cars. These are one-celled animals. Depending on the water and its contents, there may be many different organisms or a lot of the same kind. You may see:

   marine life: shrimp, paramecium euglena
   fresh water life: volvox, daphnia

9. YEAST

Cells do a lot of the same things you do. They just do it at a micro level. Yeasts are one-celled plants that breathe, eat, and excrete. Here is an experiment that will let you watch yeast breathe.

Ideas to Think About

What is yeast? Where does it live? Why is it important? Yeasts are micro-sized one-celled plants that are distant cousins of the mushroom. While most plants have chlorophyll, that green miracle substance that lets them make their own food, yeasts don't. They must turn their surroundings into food. Yeasts convert sugar into alcohol and in the process breathe out carbon dioxide gas.

Materials

Package of dry yeast, warm water, measuring cup and spoons, large bowl, funnel, sugar, salt, spoon, balloons, clean pop bottles, marker

Experiment

1. Mix the package of dry yeast with one cup of water. Stir until the yeast is dissolved.
2. Pour the liquid into three pop bottles. Pour the same amount in each bottle.
3. Label the bottles 1, 2, and 3.
4. Add the following to the bottles and mix well:
    Bottle 1: 1/4 teaspoon sugar
    Bottle 2: 1/4 teaspoon salt
    Bottle 3: nothing
5. Stretch a balloon onto the top of each bottle. Make sure the balloons are on tight.
6. Set the bottles in a bowl of warm water.
7. Predict what will happen.
8. Record what happens. What conditions did your yeasts like best?

Extensions

1. You might also want to look at yeasts under the microscope. Looking at them under the high-power scope is very frustrating because they are so small. But an adult can show yeasts with a projector scope. Smear some of the yeast solution onto a slide. View it with the projector scope. Make a drawing.

2. Yeasts can double their number in 15 minutes. Complete the pattern here for a math extension:
    • Complete the pattern to 8.
    • Predict the number of yeasts you will have after 60 minutes.
    • Write what you know about the pattern.
    • For a picture of exponential growth, graph the yeast growth.

minutes	number of yeasts
0	1
15	2
30	4

10. CELL CITY

You are a cell city. You are made of zillions of cells that have different jobs. It shouldn't be surprising that cells that do different things in a body look different. Learn about some of your different cells with this Concentration game.

Materials
Cell City card sheet, scissors, crayons or colored pencils

To Prepare the Cards
1. Name each cell on the sheet by matching those with names to those that aren't named.
2. Write down the job of each cell or an amazing fact about each.
3. Color the cell cards if you wish.
4. Cut out the cards.

To Play
1. Find a partner to play this Concentration game with.
2. Lay all the cards face down in front of you.
3. Player One turns up one card. He or she names the cell and has one try to find a matching card. If a matching card is found, Player One keeps the pair. If a matching card is not found, Player Two takes a turn to try to make the match (the first card Player One chose always remains face up).
4. The player who makes the most matches wins. The object is to remember the position of the cards and, more important, learn the names of the cells.

Cell City Concentration Cards

Cells Glossary

bacteria A very common one-celled organism.
blood tissue The cells that transport food, oxygen, and wastes.
cell The basic unit of living things.
cell membrane A thin sheet that lines the cell wall, like the skin on the inside of an eggshell. Acts like a plastic bag that filters things in and out of the cell.
cell wall The outer edge of a cell. Plants tend to have thick ones.
chlorophyll The green chemical contained in plant cells that can convert light to food.
connective tissue The cells that tie body parts together.
cytoplasm The living material of a cell (excluding the nucleus).
muscle tissue What moves and does the body's work.
nerve tissue Sends messages inside the body.
nucleus The dense area inside the cells that acts as their information center.
organ A group of tissues that work together.
organism A living thing. It can be a one-celled bacteria or a zillion-celled killer whale.
skeletal tissue Supports the body.
skin tissue Covers and protects the body, inside and out.
system A group of organs that work together.
tissue A group of the same kind of cells.
vacuoles Spaces inside a cell. Some are used for storing food.

Forces

1. BALANCING ACT

Make this cool desktop sculpture. Use it to investigate balance points. You will get a real feel for the dynamics of balance as you coax this sculpture to equilibrium.

Materials
Clay, 5 plastic straws, pencil or pen with flat top, pushpin, hole punch, four paper strips, tape, cardboard squares (optional), scissors

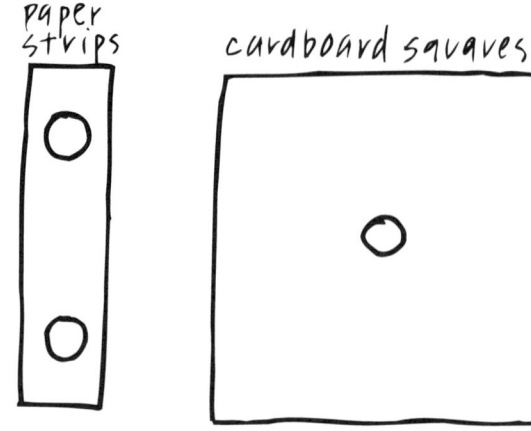

Experiment
This balancing sculpture is easiest to build from the bottom up. Assemble it first, then go back and adjust the balance.

1. Snip the tips of the straws at an angle. This makes them easier to slide through the paper-strip connectors.
2. Wrap a paper strip around the center of each straw. Tape the strips snugly in place. (The straws should move, but not easily.)
3. Punch the strips with a hole punch.
4. Assemble the straws as shown. Push a pencil point down into a ball of clay to make the stand. Pin the last straw to the eraser tip.
5. Push the straw that's pinned to the pencil into the last paper strip.
6. Adjust the paper strips until the sculpture balances. You can use cardboard squares as counterweights to help balance. Hint: Your sculpture doesn't have to balance horizontally. Shift the balance points around until you get a sculpture shape you like.

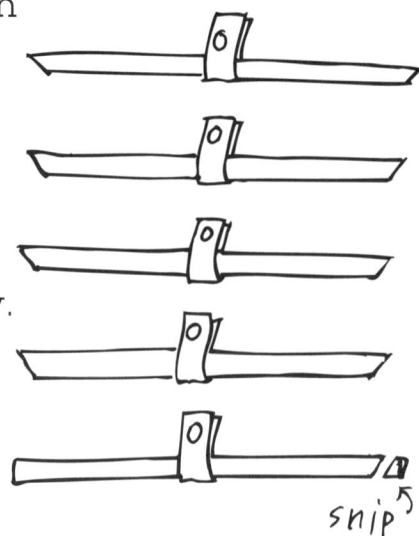

Ideas to Think About
1. What makes something balance?
2. How are the sculpture's balancing arms (the straws) like a seesaw? Can you find a pattern in the balance points? Can you get all the straws level with the floor? What do you have to do?
3. Each straw has a balance point. How can you find it?
4. A well-balanced sculpture will stand on the tip of a finger. Can you get yours to do this?

What's Happening
For a mobile to balance, the weight times the distance on one side of the fulcrum (balance point) must equal the weight times the distance on the other side (just like on a seesaw).

More to Explore
Add more balancing arms to make a bigger sculpture. (You may need a taller stand.) Use wire to attach different kinds of interesting counterweights such as colored balls of clay or doodads.

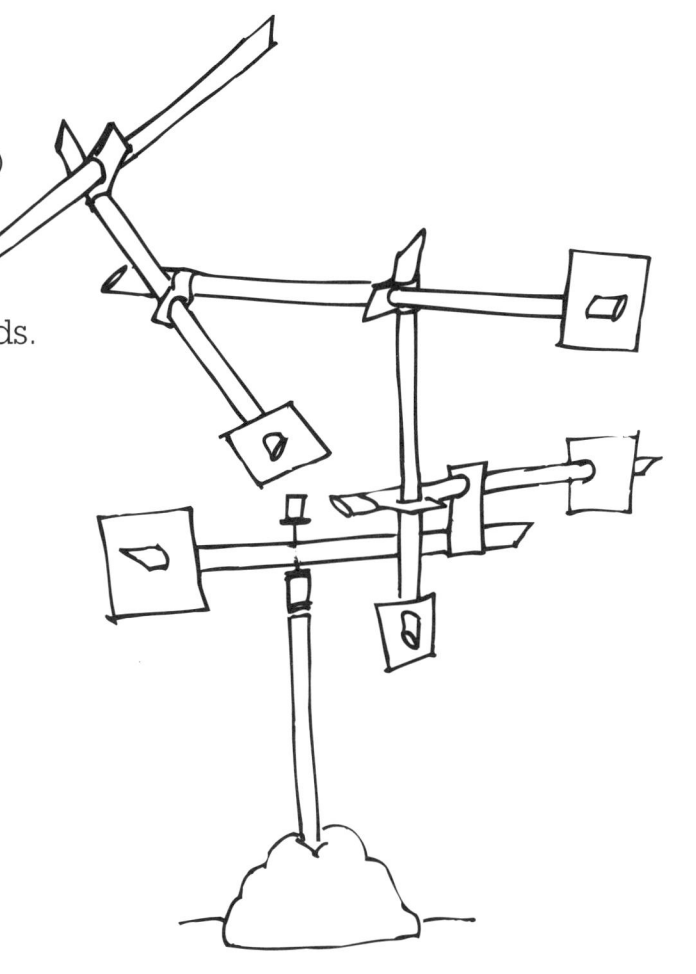

2. SEESAW SCIENCE

Experiment with a simple balance. Change the weights on each end and watch what happens. Change the distance of the weights from the center and watch what happens. Can you find a pattern? Can you predict a pattern for balance?

Materials
Balance beam, block, table, nail, paper clips, clay (if needed)

Getting Ready
1. Set the block up on the edge of a table.
2. Hang the balance beam on the nail.
3. Make sure the balance beam is level. (If it is a bit off, weight the high side with a bit of clay to make it hang level.)

Experiment
Share the balance beam with a partner. Fool around with the paper clips to find out how to get the beam to balance.

Ideas to Think About
1. How can you tell if two things weigh the same?
2. Do two paper clips always balance each other? Why not? (What do you know about teeter-totters?)
3. How does shifting weight positions along the beam change the balance?

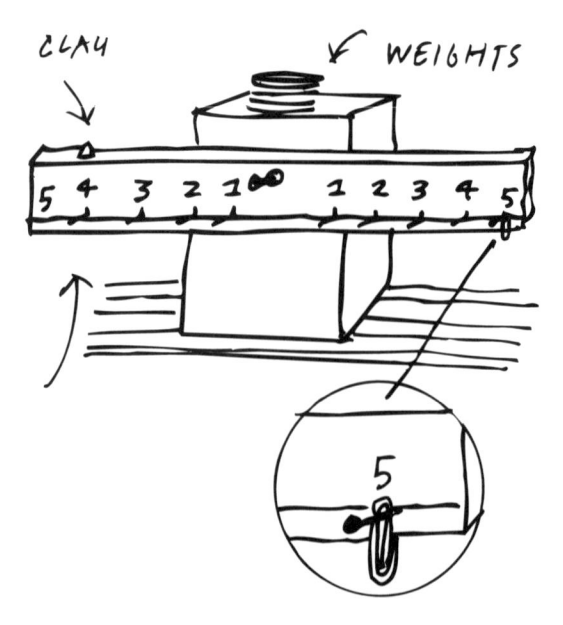

Activity
1. Place a weight on one side of the fulcrum.
2. Have your partner balance the beam by adding at least two weights on the other side.
3. If your partner succeeds, he or she gets a point.
4. Change places and try to balance the weight your partner puts on one side of the beam. Take turns for several more rounds.
5. The partner with the most points wins. The winner starts the next round.
6. As you play, record the weights and distances of the successful combinations.
7. To make the game harder, place two weights on one side of the fulcrum. Your partner must balance the beam using a different combination of two or more weights. Keep score the same way and record the results.

What's Happening
For the beam to balance, the weight-X distance on one side of the fulcrum must equal the weight-X distance on the other side (just like on a seesaw). You can write a simple math equation for this idea:

$$\text{Weight-X Distance} = \text{Weight-X Distance}$$

Plug in the number combinations collected in the game and see for yourself if the equation works.

Extensions
1. Write a description of the balance pattern.
2. Write down a dozen numbers. Work out on paper a number combination that will balance each number. Test the answers on the beam.
3. Load up all the numbers with weights. Play a take-away balance game.
4. Play a game with a partner. Choose two numbers on one side of the fulcrum. Throw dice. Your partner must use that number plus any others needed to balance the beam. (Both players start with a limited number of weights.)

3. FIND YOUR CENTER

It is easy to guess the balance point of a regular-shaped object like a ruler, but it's not so easy with an odd shape like yourself. Predict your center of balance, then use string and gravity to check your guess.

Ideas to Think About
What is a center of gravity? Where would it be on a ruler? Do you have a center of gravity? Where do you think it is?

Materials
String, washer, lightweight cardboard, pushpin, pencil, scissors, ruler

To Predict the Center
1. Cut out a human shape from lightweight cardboard.
2. Predict the cardboard person's center of gravity. Make an x with the pencil to mark the spot.
3. Make a center detector by tying a washer to the end of a piece of string.

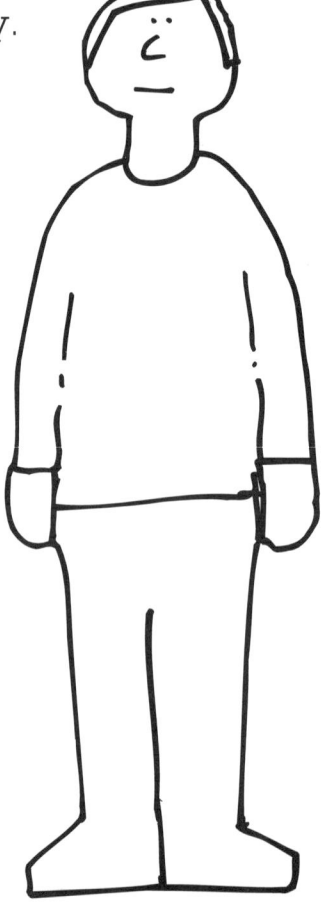

Experiment

Use the center detector to verify if your prediction was correct. Here's how:

1. Put dots in three different places on the edge of the shape.
2. Pin up the shape by sticking the pushpin through a dot. (Make sure that the hole is big enough so the shape can pivot freely. Enlarging the hole with a pencil tip will do the trick.)
3. Hang the center detector's string from the pin so the weight hangs down.
4. Draw a ruler line along the string.
5. Do steps 2, 3, and 4 for the other two dots.
6. The center of gravity is the point where the three lines intersect.
7. Test if the point you find is the true center of gravity by balancing the cardboard on that point on a pencil eraser.

More to Explore

1. Experiment with other odd shapes. Where would the center of gravity be on a dog, a cat, or another odd shape? Cut the form you choose out of lightweight cardboard. Predict its center. Then test with the center detector.
2. Try hanging over parallel bars to find your center. Would it change if you were holding a pair of bricks?

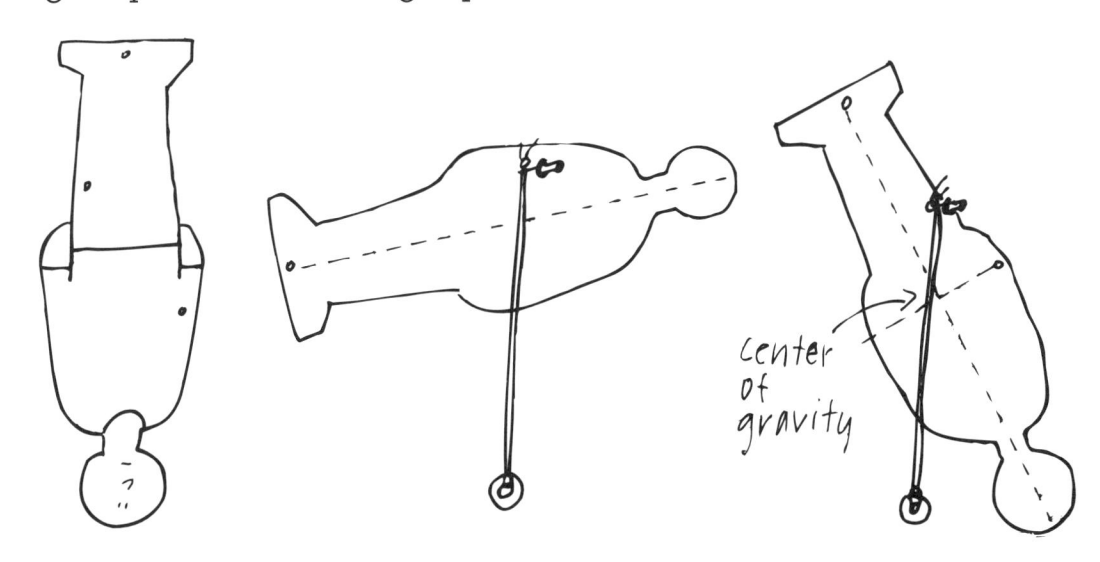

4. FIENDISH FILM CAN

The film can in these activities defies human powers. It positively refuses to be picked up! You don't believe it? Try it and see. The activities will give you a real feel for people's shifting center of gravity.

TEACHER DEMONSTRATION
The most fun way to explore these activities is to present them in front of the class. First introduce the fiendish film can. Then set up the tricks and ask for a volunteer. When he or she fails to lift the cantankerous can, dare someone else to try.

TOOTHY TRICK

Materials
Film can

Activity
1. Ask the children if anyone thinks he or she can pick up the fiendish film can from a kneeling position —without using their hands.
2. Have the volunteer kneel. Place the film can an arm's length away from the volunteer's knees.
3. Have the volunteer clasp hands behind his or her back.
4. Ask the volunteer to pick up the can with the teeth.
5. Is it too hard? Have the child try knocking the film can over with his or her nose. Warn the child not to shift so far forward that balance is lost and falling over is possible.

CHAIR LIFT

Not only does this film can refuse to be picked up, it has the power to prevent a chair from being lifted!

Materials
Wall, straight-back chair, film can

Activity
1. Set the film can on the seat of the chair.
2. Set the chair next to the wall.
3. Have the volunteer stand three foot-lengths away from the wall, forehead resting on the wall.
4. Have the child lift the film can by lifting the chair.

EASY MONEY

Announce that you have money you want to give away. All the receiver has to do is pick it up. The only hitch is that the money's in the can—the fiendish film can. Who wants to pick up a little easy money?

Materials
Film can, paper money, wall

Activity
1. Stand the volunteer against the wall.
2. Place the money in the can.
3. Place the fiendish film can about two feet away from the volunteer's toes.
4. To win the money, all the volunteer has to do is pick up the can and stand up again, making sure his or her heels stay against the wall.
5. If the child fails, offer to make it a little easier by moving the money a bit closer. Any volunteers?

TOOTHY TRICK

After the volunteer tries to pick up the can from a kneeling position, consider the following.

Ideas to Think About

If you put bricks in your back pockets, would this trick be easier to do? Do you think people with big broad shoulders would have an easier or a harder time with this stunt? Would it matter?

What's Happening

Because weight is distributed differently on different bodies, the center of gravity is different. Broad, heavy shoulders make a more top-heavy body than one with a weightier bottom. Broad-shouldered people have a harder time with this trick.

CHAIR LIFT

After the volunteer tries to pick up the can while his or her forehead is against the wall, consider the following.

What's Happening

Because the volunteer's weight is leaning so far forward, he or she doesn't have the strength to pull out of the position. The volunteer is stuck.

EASY MONEY

After the volunteer tries to pick up the money, consider the following.

Ideas to Think About

1. How do you usually lift a chair? How do you bend over to pick up something? How do you reach forward on your hands and knees? What happens to your center of gravity when you do each of these things?
2. Can you devise a test to locate your center of gravity? Can you think of a way to change it? (For instance, what if you put on lead shoes?)

What's Happening

It is IMPOSSIBLE to bend over with your back flat against a wall. As you lean forward, you automatically stick your rear end out to counterbalance yourself. The wall prevents counterbalancing, no matter how close the money is.

5. CRASH TESTING

When your center of gravity gets too far away from over your feet, you are in danger of falling. The same is true for inanimate objects. They fall when their tops tip out over their base. Experiment with ways to make tall things more stable.

STAND-UP TUBE CRASH TESTING

Materials
Typing paper, rubber bands, paper clips, tape, construction materials such as cardboard, fabric pieces, glue, etc.

Activity
1. Roll a sheet of typing paper to make a tall tube. Fasten it with a rubber band.
2. Set the tube on its end on a table top.
3. Try blowing the tube over.
4. Now alter the tube so that it can't be blown over. Work with a friend or a small group. Rules: You can add any materials and weight. However, the finished tube must be free standing (no fair taping it to the table) and the same height you started with.
5. Test the altered tube by trying to blow it over. Try the experiment again with other tubes.

Ideas to Think About
1. Did any of the tubes survive the blow-hard test? Which tubes were the most stable?
2. Make a list of what creates stability. The list might include adding weight at the bottom, having a wide base, changing the shape of the tube.

NOTEBOOK-PAPER TOWER CRASH TESTING

Use what you learned about stability in the previous activity to build notebook-paper towers.

Materials
Tape, 15 sheets of notebook paper

Activity
1. Work in a team of two to four to build the tallest notebook-paper tower possible.
2. You may use only 15 sheets of notebook paper and tape to build your tower. The finished tower must stand for at least 10 seconds.

More to Explore
1. The Leaning Tower of Pisa has been leaning for centuries. Can you tell what keeps it from falling by looking at a picture of it?
2. How far can you lean over before you topple?

Extension
Stack up a tower of books stair-step fashion (each book is set back a little from the edge of the one below it). Is there a limit to how many you can stack? Does how you stack the books make a difference? Can you predict what conditions must be present to make the stack fall?

6. TIPSY TRIANGLE

Can you balance a triangle on its tip? Cut one out from cardboard and see if it can be done. Get a feel for throwing some weight around. You will discover some things about gravity in the process.

Ideas to Think About
Did you ever have a baby cup that tipped back up every time you tipped it over? Or one of those knock-down clowns that stood up every time you punched it over? How do these toys work? Can you think of any other toys that work the same way?

What's Happening
These toys are made with a lot of weight at the bottom. The force of gravity pulls more strongly on the part of the toy with the most weight (or mass). The toy rolls until the weight is pulled to the lowest point. Moral: Mass (or weight) likes to get down.

Materials
Lightweight cardboard, coins, tape or glue stick, scissors, paper, pencil

Experiment #1
1. Cut a triangle from lightweight cardboard.
2. Create a way to stand the triangle on its tip. Experiment. You may need some outside props. Hint: Think about how you can change the balance point of an object by changing where the object is weighted.
3. How did you solve the problem? Record your favorite solutions. Did you think of giving your triangle a counterweighted tail?

Ideas to Think About
What position is the most stable for a triangle?

76 Table-Top Science: Intermediate ©1997 Monday Morning Books, Inc.

What's Happening

A triangle won't stand on its tip because it has a narrow base. Also, most of the weight is at the wide end. Gravity is always pulling the weight down so the triangle falls off its tip.

Experiment #2

1. For a toy that seems to defy the laws of gravity, give your triangle a crescent-shaped tail. Begin by tracing a crescent shape onto a piece of paper.
2. Glue the shape onto lightweight cardboard.
3. Cut out the tail.
4. Cut slits through the tip of the triangle, big enough to accommodate the tail.
5. Slide the tail in place.
6. Counterweight the tail by gluing or taping two coins on the tail's tip.
7. Stand your triangle on its tip.

Ideas to Think About

1. Why does the tipsy triangle suddenly balance? Hint: What happened to the center of gravity?
2. What happens when you remove the coins? How do the coins keep the triangle standing? Hint: Think about how animals use their tails. What do animal tails have in common with the tipsy triangle tail?

What's Happening

Adding a weighted tail lowers the center of gravity, making the triangle stable.

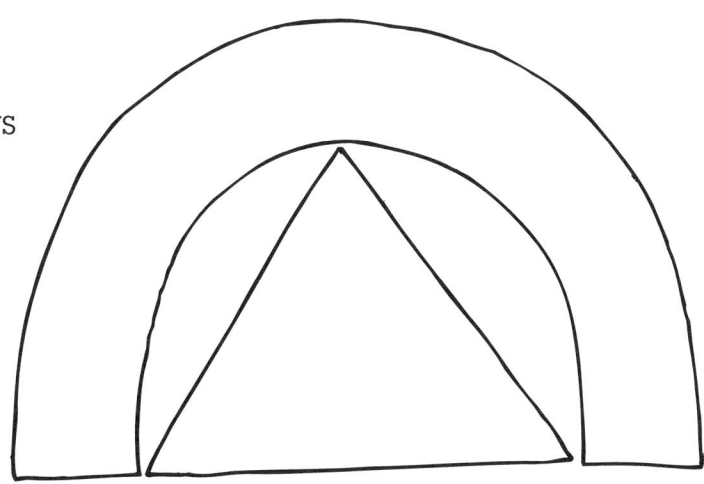

7. A BALANCED LUNCH

You've heard of eating a balanced lunch, but have you ever actually balanced your lunch? Here are a number of strange and wonderful balancing stunts using fruits and vegetables and kitchen items. Build some "balanced lunches" with whatever materials you have—there's no need to follow each stunt exactly. Then invent some of your own.

SPUD-TACULAR

Materials
Small potatoes, metal forks, table, ruler (optional)

Experiment
1. Work in a group. Put the materials you need at a station along with the picture shown here.
2. Connect the forks with the potatoes. Join them in a way that makes a curve.
3. Stand the curve on the edge of a table or on a ruler sticking out of a drawer.

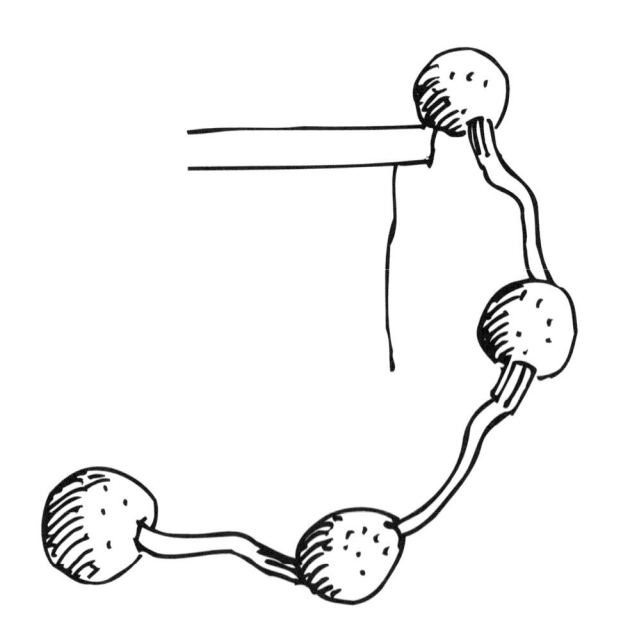

FLYING ZUCCHINI

Materials
Zucchini squash, orange or tangerine, toothpick, two metal forks, table knife, tall bottle

Experiment
1. Work in a group. Put the materials you need at a station along with the picture shown here.
2. Cut the zucchini in half. Set aside the stem end.
3. Cut the other chunk in half again.
4. Stick forks on either side of the big chunk. The forks need to point backward like wings.
5. Push the small chunks onto the tip of each fork.
6. Attach the tangerine to the stem end with a toothpick.
7. Set it on the edge of a bottle so the zucchini "flies." Hint: Adjust the weights by moving the forks. Try using a bigger or smaller tangerine.

CARROT STAND

Materials
Carrot, potato, coat hanger wire (the lightweight, flexible kind is best), pliers

Experiment
1. Work in a group. Put the materials you need at a station along with the picture shown here.
2. Open the coat hanger wire (pliers will help).
3. Bend the wire into a curve.
4. Make a loop at one end of the curve. Attach the carrot so it doesn't wiggle.
5. Attach a potato counterweight to the other end.
6. Stand the carrot on its tip. Hint: Adjust the curve and the counterweight to get the carrot onto its tip.

APPLE ACROBAT

Materials
Apple, two forks, weights (tangerine, clay balls, potatoes), toothpick, bottle (slim and tall)

Experiment
1. Work in a group. Put the materials you need at a station along with the picture shown here.
2. Stick the toothpick in the center of the apple, heavy side down.
3. Stick the forks into opposite sides of the apple, handles down.
4. Weight the handles.
5. Balance the apple on its toothpick using the bottle as a stand.
6. Adjust the weights so the apple balances. Hint: Standing the creation on a fingertip first will help you get a feel for adjusting the balance.

Extensions
1. Use things from around the house to make an even stranger balancing creation.
2. Write about your favorite balancing trick. Draw it, then describe how you think the weights hold it in position.

8. FLYING CAT

Use coins as counterweights to make a different kind of paper balance toy—a flying cat! Then get your cat to balance on the overhead "high wire." For a little extra fun, try creating your own shape that can hang from the high wire.

Materials
Lightweight cardboard, flying cat shape (copied on a copy machine or traced onto paper), coins, tape or glue stick, markers, string, scissors, two chairs

Experiment
1. Tape or paste the cat shape to the cardboard.
2. Color it, then cut the cat out.
3. To set up the tightrope, cut a long string and tie it between the backs of two chairs. (An overhead string stretched across the room would be even more spectacular.)
4. Counterweight the cat with the coins. (Balance the cat on the tip of your finger first to help you decide where to stick the coins.)
5. When the cat balances, move it to the high wire.

What's Happening
Flying cats work on the same principle as the tipsy triangle. When weights are added to the cat's feet, its center of gravity is lowered. When the center of gravity is low, objects become more stable and balance more easily.

More to Explore
Use what you learned about counterweights to make a different balance toy of your own. Be sure to give it wings or arms so that enough weight can be added to make it balance on the string.

Table-Top Science: Intermediate ©1997 Monday Morning Books, Inc.

9. ACROBAT

Apply what you learned about balance and equilibrium when you make this clothespin man.

Materials
Pinch clothespins, stiff but bendable wire (16-18 gauge), plasticine clay, markers, tape measure, wire cutter, pliers

Activity
1. Use the markers to decorate the clothespin to look like a man.
2. Cut a 16-inch (40 cm) length of wire.
3. Twist one end of the wire around the neck of the clothespin man.
4. Using pliers, tighten the twists so the wire won't slip off the clothespin. Ask an adult for help if you need it.
5. Bend the wire down to the clothespin man's waist and then out.
6. Now make the man stand up straight on the edge of a table top. Hint: Start by adding a clay weight to the end of the wire.

Ideas to Think About
Does your acrobat stand straight or is it cockeyed? What makes the difference? What effect will adding more weight have? Predict. Then test. Note: If you are artistic, you might want to make your clay counterweights fish shaped instead of ball shaped.

Table-Top Science: Intermediate ©1997 Monday Morning Books, Inc.

10. FALLING BODIES

Discover more about the physics of falling bodies with these two experiments. The first is a classic. With it, Galileo changed the course of science forever.

ORANGE VS. GRAPEFRUIT DROP

Materials
An orange and a grapefruit or other light and heavy bodies such as a tennis ball and a basketball, a marble and a bowling ball

Ideas to Think About
Pick up the orange and the grapefruit or two other things. What do you notice about them—their size, weight, and so on? Think about dropping them from exactly the same height at exactly the same time. Which will fall faster? Why do you think so?

Experiment
1. Drop the two things simultaneously.
2. Watch closely. What happens? Surprised?
3. Ask a friend to do the same experiment. Then try it from a greater height. Try it with different light and heavy bodies.

What's Happening
The orange and the grapefruit hit the ground at the same time. The same goes for a tennis ball and a bowling ball. Bodies fall at the same rate, no matter what they weigh.

PAPER AND BOOK DROP

Materials
A sheet of paper, a book

Activity
Predict what will happen when you drop a sheet of paper and a book at the same time from the same height. Test your prediction. What happens? Why?

What's Happening
The book hits the floor first. The resistance (friction) of the air tends to slow down lightweight objects with large surfaces such as the sheet of paper.

More to Explore
1. What will happen if you crumple the sheet of paper before you drop it? Predict and try it.
2. What will happen if you put the sheet of paper on top of the book and drop them together? Predict and try it.
3. Work with a partner. Try dropping pairs of things like a paper cup and a pencil. Predict what will happen. Record your results. Write an explanation of your results.
4. Think about which will fall faster—a pound of feathers or a pound of gold. What weighs more—a pound of feathers or a pound of gold?

Extensions
1. Read about Galileo (look for books in the library). Make a list of 10 interesting things about him.
2. With one or more friends, write a rap or song about Galileo. Use a tune you like and include interesting things you learned about him in your research.

11. BUMPER SLUMPER

Falling, like everything on Earth, is affected by friction. In this activity, falling and friction interact to make a goofy, kinetic toy. Make a Bumper Slumper, then use it to investigate the effects of less or more friction.

Materials

Clay, wire, wire cutter, wood dowel, cardboard, doodads (wiggly or noisy things to attach to your Bumper Slumper for fun, such as a film can filled with beans, or colored tissue paper strips)

To Make the Bumper Slumper

1. Fix the dowel in a clay base so it stands up. Set the clay on a piece of cardboard.
2. Wind a length of wire around the end of the dowel. Leave a few centimeters sticking out.
3. Press a ball of clay on the wire's end.
4. Raise the twisted wire to the top of the dowel and let it drop.
5. Adjust the wire (tighten or loosen it) so you get a bumping action as it falls.
6. If you have trouble getting your Bumper Slumper to bump, share ideas with a friend.

Experiment

1. Time the falls of the Bumper Slumper. If you can, work with a group and time all the Bumper Slumpers.
2. List the properties of a fast faller and a slow faller. Anything in common? How does more or less friction affect the falling time?

Table-Top Science: Intermediate ©1997 Monday Morning Books, Inc.

More to Explore

Work with the Bumper Slumper to make it do different things:
- Fall in the slowest time possible
- Fall with a set number of bounces, say a dozen
- Fall for a specific length of time (like 15 seconds)
- Fall with the fewest bounces top to bottom
- Fall with the most noise and motion—make it the wildest-looking thing you can create

Test all your creations. Then write about how you accomplished your goals.

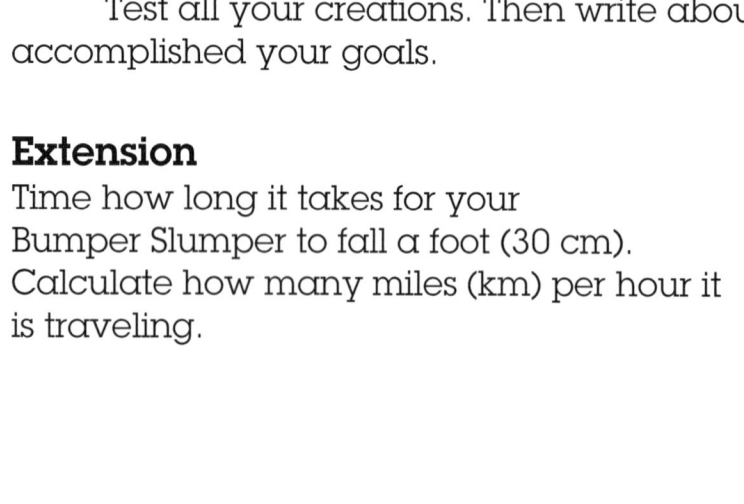

Extension

Time how long it takes for your Bumper Slumper to fall a foot (30 cm). Calculate how many miles (km) per hour it is traveling.

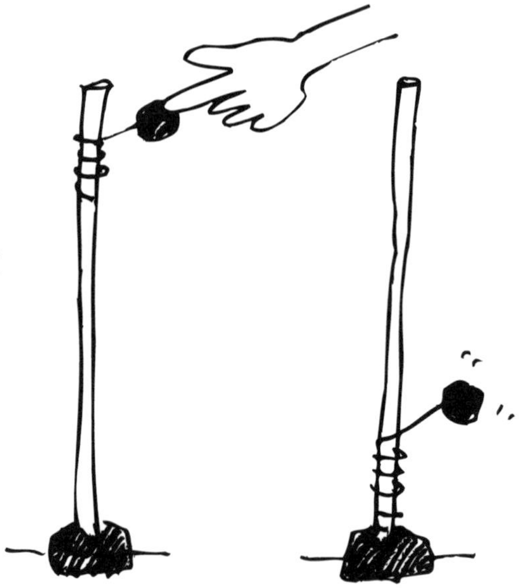

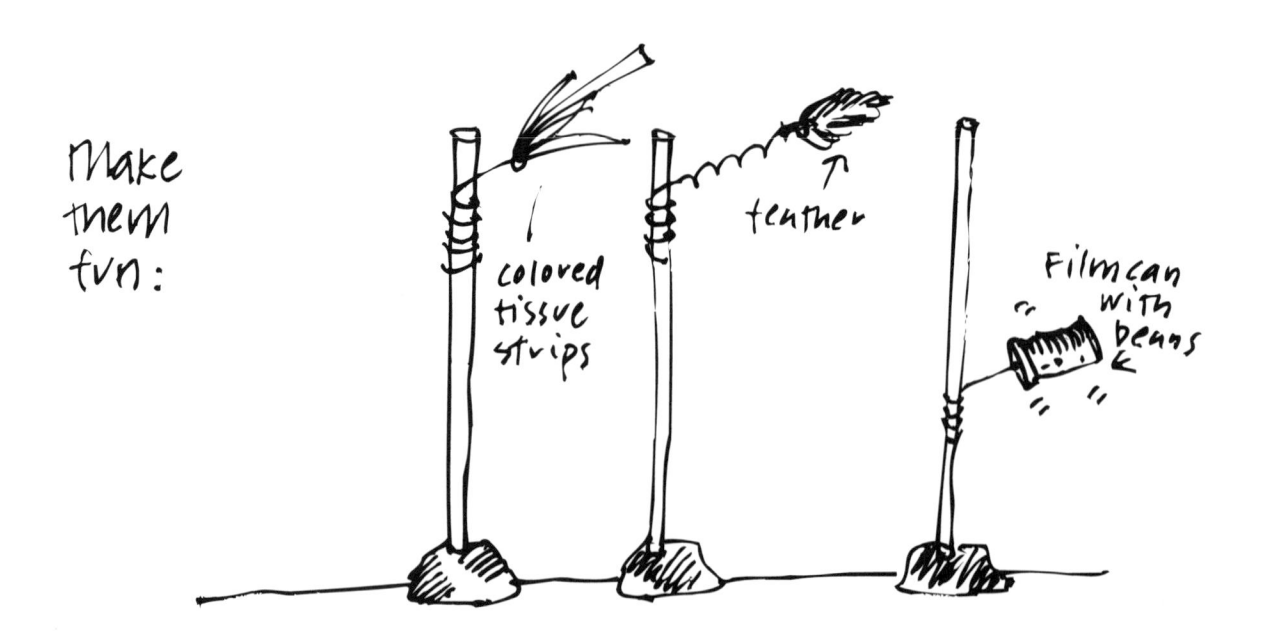

Make them fun:

colored tissue strips

feather

Film can with beans

Cause and Effect Testing

Predict, then test what happens when you:

Stretch the length of wire

Shrink the length of wire

Tighten the coil

Loosen the coil

Even out the coil

Make the coil uneven

Change the coil material

Change the dowel material

Change the angle of the dowel

Other changes

12. FRICTION TESTING

Use this simple method for guessing and testing the effects of friction on different materials. Graph the results.

Materials
Wooden block, pushpins, string, scissors, paper clips, washers, testing materials such as sections of waxed paper, sandpaper, foil, straws, sticks, rubber bands, etc. (use your imagination)

To Make the Tester
1. Cut yard (meter)-long lengths of string.
2. Tie a paper clip to the end of the string. Bend it open so you can hang washers on it.
3. Use a pushpin to attach the string and weight to the block of wood.
4. Set the block about a foot from the table edge. Hang the weight over the edge of the table.

To Test the Effects of Friction
1. Put a layer of material under the block.
2. Hang one washer weight on the clip. Bump the table with your fist to overcome inertia. Inertia is the tendency of matter at rest to remain at rest and for matter in motion to remain at motion.
3. No movement? Add another weight. Bump again.
4. Continue to add weights until the block moves.
5. Record the results.

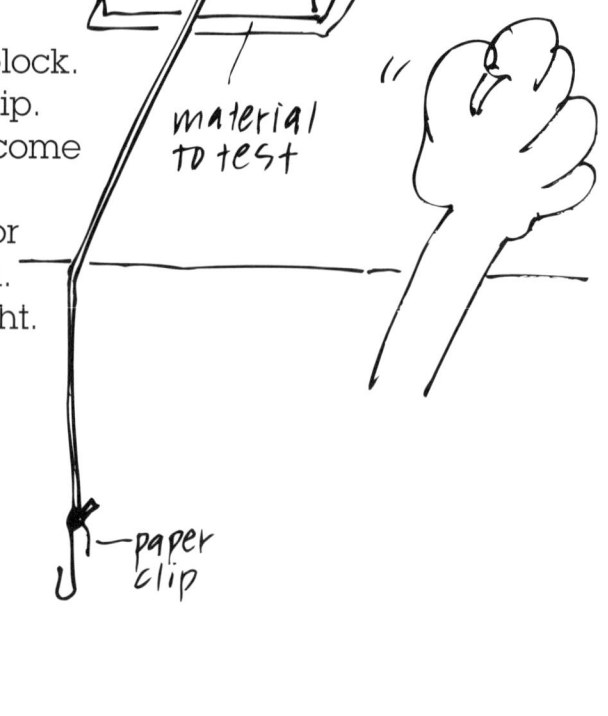

Activity
1. Work in a team. Select at least six materials.
2. Predict which material will create the most friction. Predict which will create the least.
3. Put each material under the block and test it. Record the results.
4. How did your predictions compare to your results?

Extensions
1. Discover the most friction-free surface.
2. Determine the friction champion (no fair using glue).
3. Invent a tape tester—a device that can test tape's friction factor. Discover which tape is the stickiest one of all.

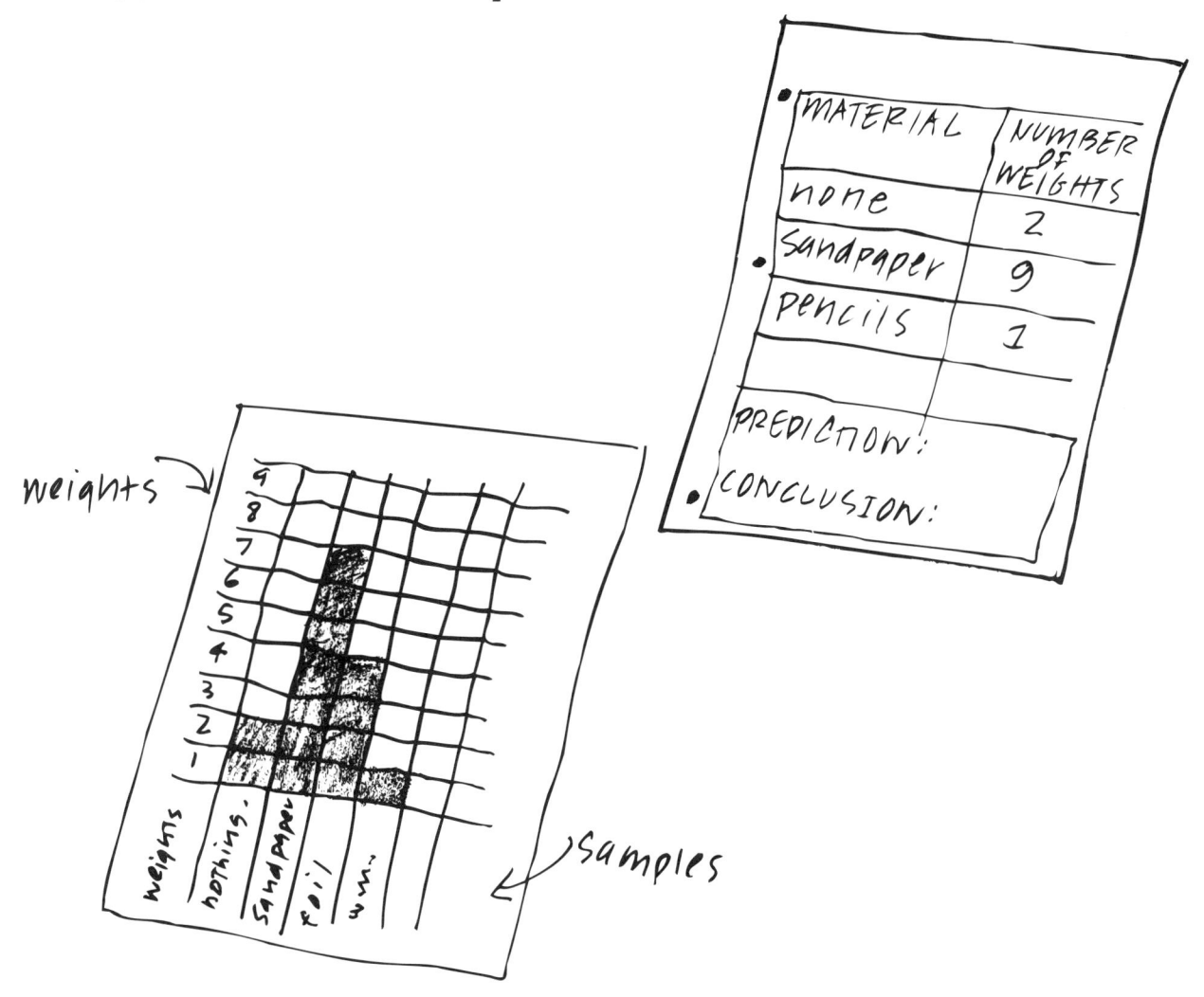

13. INERTIA CHALLENGES

These stunts seem like magic—but the tricks really rely on the force of inertia. They are fun to do and fun to master. Think of them as good starting places for noticing how inertia works in everyday life.

TEACHER DEMONSTRATION

Set up the four following challenges in stations. Demonstrate each challenge and show the goal, but let the children discover their own methods for meeting each challenge. Let them know that with practice it is definitely possible to do each stunt.

COIN DROP

Materials
Coin, index card or heavy paper, glass, scissors

Setup
1. Cut a four-inch (10 cm) square from the index card.
2. Place the square on top of the glass.
3. Set the coin in the middle of the card.

Challenge
To drop the coin into the glass without touching the coin.

THE LOOP

Materials
Stiff paper (manila folder weight), penny, glass, tape, scissors, ruler

Setup
1. Cut out a strip of stiff paper one inch wide by eight inches (2.5 cm x 20 cm) long.
2. Tape the ends together to make a loop.
3. Set the loop on top of the glass. Place the coin on top of the loop.

Challenge
To knock the loop out of the way so the coin falls into the glass.

KARATE CHOP

Materials
Pen with a flat top, ball of clay, writing paper, scissors, coin, ruler, table

Setup
1. Cut a paper strip one inch wide and eight inches (2.5 cm x 20 cm) long.
2. Place the ball of clay near the edge of a table.
3. Stand the pen in the clay ball with the flat side up.
4. Place the end of the paper strip on the pen. Hold it in place with the coin on top.

Challenge
To remove the paper without disturbing the coin.

TOWER TAKE-DOWN

Materials
Stack of coins or checkers, tray with sides

Setup
1. Stack the coins or checkers into a tower.
2. Put the tower into the tray.

Challenge
To take down the tower by removing the bottom coin one at a time.

slide the ruler along the tray's surface.

INERTIA CHALLENGES HINTS

Copy these hints onto cards. Instead of mentioning them during the demonstrations, leave the appropriate card at each station for the children to use as they experiment.

Coin Drop Hints
The trick is to strike the card with a strong sideways force. Flicking the card with your longest finger is best. Also make sure the card has smooth edges so it slips from under the coin.

The Loop Hints
The secret is to flick the loop away by hitting it on the inside. This bends the loop down and out of the way rather than forcing it up and disturbing the coin.

Karate Chop Hints
The coin will remain at rest if you strike the paper in a fast, downward motion. Striking it with the edge of a ruler is easier than using your fingers.

Tower Take-down Hints
The trick is to hit the bottom coin hard with a sideways force. Flicking the penny with a finger is one way. Some have better luck giving the penny a hard push with a strip of flexible cardboard.

Ideas to Think About
What challenge was hardest? the easiest? Why? Were there any secrets that you learned? Explain how you think inertia works in each of the stunts.

What's Happening
In each of these stunts, the force of inertia acts to keep the coins in their place. A sharp, sideways blow to each base moves it out of the way. Meanwhile, inertia keeps the coin resting in place. When the base disappears, the force of gravity pulls the resting coin downward.

More to Explore
1. Make a list of at least three places where you feel or see the force of inertia in your world. Write or tell what inertia is doing in one of the places. Consider: in the car, pushing or pulling a shopping cart, roller skating, biking.
2. Explain why "inertia belts" would be a good name for car seat belts.

14. THE GREAT SLOW RACE

Win this race by making a marble drop down a ramp as slowly as possible. Use any method you can think of. Are you ready? Get set! Slow!

Ideas to Think About
Try this: Drop a marble a foot (30 cm) off the ground and watch it fall to the ground. Drop the same marble down a ramp that's a foot (30 cm) high. Notice that the marble takes longer to fall down the ramp, even though it is falling the same distance downwards. What might make the marble move faster or slower down the ramp?

Materials
Cardboard, scissors, watch with a second hand (a stopwatch is best), glue, tape or pins, ruler, construction materials

Building the Raceway
Design a slow-falling marble raceway. Experiment with what you know about friction and the steepness of slopes to slow its drop.
1. Cut out a 12" by 12" (30 cm x 30 cm) cardboard square. Cut out several 12" by 1/2" (30 cm x 1 cm) cardboard ramps.
2. Use tape or pins to attach a ramp to the square.
3. Send your marble down the ramp to test the fall.
4. Experiment with ways to make your marble go slower, following the Slow Race Rules.

The Slow Race Rules
1. Make your marble fall for as many seconds as possible.
2. If you race with other slow racers, make sure everyone uses only 12" x 12" (30 cm x 30 cm) pieces of cardboard and the same size marbles.
3. No ramp may stick out beyond the cardboard back.
4. Every marble must stay in continuous motion (no nudges).
5. Experiment: any ramp and any materials are OK to use.

Holding the Race
1. Time each marble fall. If you are playing with other racers, record each contestant's name and times.
2. Write down how long the longest fall took.
3. Make a list of characteristics of slow mazes and fast mazes.

More to Explore
Write about how you might redesign your maze to slow the marble down even more. If you're interested, try another round of races with several friends using your redesign ideas.

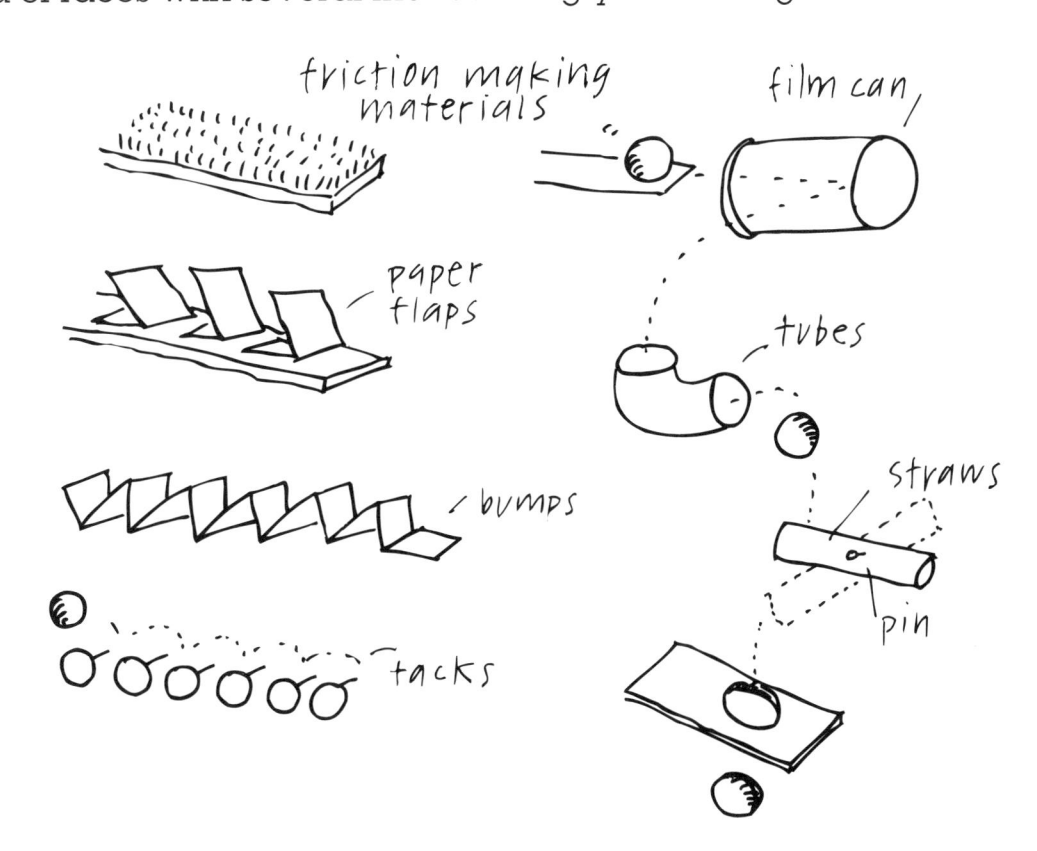

- friction making materials
- film can
- paper flaps
- tubes
- bumps
- straws
- pin
- tacks

Forces Glossary

balance A device for weighing. A beam or lever balanced exactly in the center.
balanced When the forces on one side equal the forces on the other.
balance point The point in the center of the balance. Also called the fulcrum.
center of gravity The point in any object around which all its weight centers.
density The ratio of volume to mass.
equilibrium A steady state where all forces are balanced.
force A push or a pull, a squeeze or a stretch. A force moves things.
friction A force that resists the motion of objects. When two surfaces rub together they make friction.
fulcrum The support or balance point of a lever.
gravity A force that is always pulling any two lumps of matter in the universe towards each other. Earth's gravity is always pulling you toward its center. Another name for the pull of gravity is weight. Note: The pull of gravity is different on different planets. On the moon, the pull of gravity is only 1/6 (.16) what it is on Earth. If you weighed 100 pounds (45 kg) on Earth, you would weigh less than 17 pounds (7.7 kg) on the moon. Your mass (the amount of stuff you are) would stay the same, but your weight would change.
inertia The tendency of matter to remain at rest. If the matter is in motion, inertia is the tendency to remain in motion (unless it's acted on by some other force).
mass The amount of stuff in an object. Mass is measured in pounds and ounces.
speed The distance that something moves in a unit of time.
weight The measure of the force of gravity. Weight indicates how hard gravity is pulling an object or a person toward the center of the Earth. We measure weight in pounds and ounces.